MW00677443

The Financial

Guide For

Veterinarians

Ethan Dawe

The Financial Guide for Veterinarians

The Financial Guide for Veterinarians

© 2016 All rights reserved

Publisher: Dawe's Original, LLC

The copyright laws of the United States and other countries protect content of this book.

ISBN: 978-0-578-18083-0

Cover by Richardson Media

No part of this publication may be reproduced or transmitted in any form or by any means, mechanical or electronic, including photocopying and recording, or by any information Storage and retrieval system, without permission in writing from author or publisher (Except by a reviewer, who may quote brief passages and or show brief video clips for review.)

The Financial Guide for Veterinarians

Acknowledgements

There are so many people who have influenced my life and added value to my financial acumen.

I am so grateful to my father Darryl Dawe, for instilling in me the value of hard work and paying attention to the small details. I miss him everyday.

My wife Mirinda has been instrumental in bringing this book to reality. She has been my friend, my helper and my greatest asset. Without her I would not be the man that I am today.

I have learned so much about how money truly works from several people over the last 20 plus years. Most of those people have no idea how much they have impacted my financial knowledge.

Don Blanton, founder of Money Trax / Circle of Wealth, has been instrumental in teaching me how to explain strategy to clients. Phil Cavender has given me priceless guidance on how to explain what we do for our clients.

My dear friends Tommy White, Mitch White, Chad Prewett, Benny Alaniz, Jupe Etheridge, Russ Brown and Mike Richardson mean so much to me. My dad used to say that if you have one true friend in your life, you have your share- and if you have two true friends, you have someone else's. I have seven men that I am unable to do without their friendship. I love you guys.

Dr. Robyn Wilborn has helped make my relationship with Auburn University College of Veterinary Medicine possible. I am incredibly grateful to you.

Dr. Hank Lee and Dr. Lacey Lee have been so gracious to allow me to do their planning for many years. In so many ways they have been instrumental in my growth as a consultant within the veterinary community. I am so thankful for their support and friendship.

To the hundreds of students who have shared their financial life with me in hopes that I could be of some assistance - Thank You.

More than anything else, I am thankful to my Lord and Savior, Jesus Christ, for all that He allows me. John 14:6.

One of the great pleasures that I have in this life is sharing what I know and helping people. I have found the veterinary profession to be full of high quality people and I am grateful to be a small part of this industry.

'Ethan quickly became a critical node in all of my life event planning after seeing him interact with veterinary students at Auburn University's College of Veterinary Medicine. His compassion, understanding of tax advantaged financial planning, and his ability to turn complex situations into manageable pieces has proved invaluable to hundreds of veterinary professionals, both through his interaction as a student financial planner and as a highly regarded lecturer for the Alabama Veterinary Medical Association. His knowledge of business and his extensive experience working with veterinarians and veterinary hospitals meld together to make him one of the most powerful voices in veterinary financial planning and wealth management. His message is so relevant and crucial that I place him in front of students and veterinarians at every opportunity, particularly in leadership and professional development programs for our Association.
I'm blessed to call Ethan a friend, a personal wealth management partner and the reason I can retire when I choose!'

— Bradley M. Fields, DVM, MPH, CPH, DACVPM

American Association of Small Ruminant Practitioners, Executive Director
Alabama Veterinary Medical Foundation, Executive Director
Alabama Veterinary Medical Association, Asst. Executive Director
Tiger Oak Management, LLC, CEO & Senior Veterinarian
Office Phone/Fax: 334-521-OAKS (6257)

The Financial Guide for Veterinarians

"We started using Ethan as our consultant in 2006 and he has become a dear family friend. Since that time, he has helped us with almost every facet of our personal and business finances. He has provided us with advice on Wills, asset protection, business structure, all insurances, retirement planning, investments, how to hold title to property, estate planning and so much more. His knowledge in the veterinary world is an invaluable asset to have at our disposable with just a phone call. He is always available to help and there hasn't been a major financial decision in the last 10 years that Ethan hasn't been involved in.

Ethan is someone I can strongly recommend to anyone in the veterinary profession."

— Dr. Hank Lee & Dr. Lacey Lee, Lee Veterinary Clinic, PC.

The Financial Guide for Veterinarians

Table of Contents

Chapter 1

INTRODUCTION

Over the past several years I have met one-on-one with hundreds of veterinary students, associates and practice owners. I have found that from the first year student, to the seasoned veterinarian, you all have a lot of the same questions. I am writing this book to share with you answers to some of those common questions, as well as many things that I have been talking about with veterinarians over the years. My hope is that this book will fill the void that is much needed in the veterinary community.

My goal for writing this is to help you throughout your decision making process. Specifically, I want to help you be able to think through what is best each time you are faced with financial decisions. It is important that you learn how to make *educated* decisions when dealing with your hard earned money. Most people go through life making decisions based on *emotion*. "How does this decision make me *feel?*" But 'educated you' makes the right decision far more often than 'emotional you.'

Many years ago I received a phone call from a client's good friend. This gentleman said that he had been talking with my client and understood that I would be able to help him with his finances. During that conversation he said that he felt like he had a financial problem, but was unsure of what was really going on and asked if I could take a look. Once I got into his finances I realized that he did indeed have a big problem. Although he earned just under $1 million dollars per year, he was spending almost $7000 *per month more* than he made! When I tell this story to individuals or groups they all have the same question: **How** do you do that? My answer is always the same- it's pretty easy, no matter your income level, if you do not have a way to keep up with your monthly expenses.

When I start working with a client my intention is to help them make decisions that are based on what we can verify. In this process, I educate them on their options. We discuss the pros and cons of each option in detail. Remember, I do not want anyone making decisions based on *emotion*. When you make decisions based on emotion you tend to make mistakes.

I think it would be good to give you some background on my personal history, as well as personal and business experience.

Growing up, my dad worked for a small chain of convenience stores as a supervisor. Our family was not very well off and struggled financially. When I was in the ninth grade my dad decided to take the risk of business ownership and mortgage everything we owned. He bought an old service station on the edge of town in Atmore, Alabama. We remodeled that building and opened a convenience store of our own called The Village Merchant. My dad told me later in life that we had $300 dollars left in our checking account when he opened the first store. Over the next six or seven years my dad successfully opened 10 stores with the help of three business partners. At age 49 he sold his share of the business to his partners and became an instant multi-millionaire. Of course, he had yet to pay income taxes on that sale. The following April 15th he paid approximately 50% in state and federal income taxes. **Half.**

Around that time my dad had purchased a piece of property outside of our town and built a nice home. I am sure that he expected to work on the land and enjoy the fruits of his labor for many years in retirement. But less than two years after retiring, on a Sunday afternoon while working out in the yard, my dad passed away from a heart attack. It was a defining moment in my young life.

A few weeks after the funeral I received a letter from the Internal Revenue Service that did not say 'we are sorry for your loss' or 'tough break about your dad.' Instead, it said that our family had nine months from the date of death to pay the *estate taxes* due on my dad's estate.

When the dust settled our family paid approximately 50% in *estate taxes* on what had been left over from the approximately 50% of *income taxes* that were taken less than two years earlier when he sold his company. It was at that moment that I developed a true hatred for paying taxes. Specifically, paying taxes *unnecessarily*. At the time I owned a small wholesale company and very shortly after my dad passed away, I began studying how to prevent this type of assault from happening to my family when I pass away.

I now know there are things within the tax code that are clearly allowed that can greatly reduce estate taxes. There are also several sections in the tax code, which if implemented correctly into a proper retirement investment strategy, can prevent many of the taxes that we pay each year.

Since 2005, I have successfully set up 'tax advantaged' retirement accounts for my clients. I am well versed in basic estate planning, as well as very advanced estate planning. If my father had put proper planning in place, our family could have avoided paying unnecessary taxes. When I wake up each morning my goal is to serve God, provide for my family, and teach clients how to legally avoid unnecessary taxes.

You may be wondering how this all translates into me being involved within the veterinary community. Prior to 2008, I had a handful of veterinary clients that I provided varying degrees of retirement planning and financial services for. Then in the spring of 2008 I was invited to speak to the Auburn University College of Veterinary Medicine VBMA chapter. (Veterinary Business Management Association) My first presentation to the Auburn VBMA chapter was in August of that year. Then in 2009, with the guidance of Dr. Robyn Wilborn, I helped create a 2nd year elective called 'Preparing For Your Financial Future'. In this class we cover some of the most common challenges students come across as they move from the classroom into the real world. Many of those are covered in this book. Around the same time that I started helping with the elective, I also started receiving requests from students to answer their specific questions and concerns. All of this exposure and interaction with students at Auburn University College of Veterinary Medicine led to a program that now has me available to Auburn and Tuskegee veterinary students on a regular basis.

In the fall of 2014 I helped pilot a new style of Practice Management rotation for 4th year veterinary students at Auburn University College of Veterinary Medicine. Early on we branded this rotation as the 'Practice Management Group' and have worked hard to establish this special elective rotation as not only an educational experience, but also an outreach to the Auburn veterinary community. This is also a resource for past participants. The rotation was patterned after a similar program that the University of Georgia had implemented a few years earlier, based on the efforts and direction of Mr. Jeff Sanford. Jeff has put together an exceptional program at UGA veterinary college and their pharmacy school. I cannot say enough about how much Jeff was instrumental in helping get the Practice Management rotation off the ground at AUCVM.

My knowledge of, and interaction with, the veterinary community continues to grow. I have been invited to speak at several veterinary colleges throughout the Southeast. I have given the legal/financial continuing education to the state of Alabama veterinarians via the ALVMA, as well as participated in a program for the GVMA called Power of 10. I have also provided multiple feasibility studies and evaluation reports for Auburn University College of Veterinary Medicine.

Over the past several years I have met with hundreds of veterinary students and practicing veterinary associates from all over America, as well as dozens of practice owners. I have developed what I believe to be a unique perspective and knowledge base of where a veterinary student is emotionally and financially, as well as where they want to be in 1, 3 and 5 years in the future. I hope to convey to you some of the knowledge and experience that I have collected and hopefully answer questions that you may be challenged with yourself.

There are several common questions, themes, concerns, and situations that arise in my student meetings. One theme that I have found to be true in almost every meeting is that the student is at a point in their life where they still want their parent's *opinions,* but they no longer want their parent's *advice.* It comes across as: 'I am ready for my parents to stop telling me what to do!' I believe that I have the experience to fill the void for veterinary students and that is exactly what I intend on doing with this book. As I have said many times before, I want you to be able to make educated decisions- not decisions based on emotions- and I am going to show you how to do that.

I would like to ask you to set aside and suspend what you think you know to be true about financial planning, investing, paying off debt and planning for retirement. While reading this book I only ask that you are open to new concepts, new ideas and the *possibility* that some of the things you think you know to be true…may in fact not be true at all.

To paraphrase Don Blanton:

All that you know fits comfortably inside your box of knowledge. As you move through life you will eventually come in contact with someone who has new information, or solid information, that conflicts with what is in your box of knowledge. You have two options. You can disregard this new information or *you can get a bigger box.*

I intend to challenge many of the ideas that are considered common knowledge in the financial world. It is my belief that what is considered "common knowledge" regarding financial planning is largely incorrect and/or outdated. I strongly believe that what has become "traditional financial planning" does not work in today's America.

When working with clients I like to use analogies to convey certain financial concepts. I often use the analogy of how building a house is similar to building your 'financial house'- they both must start out the same way! Your investments and retirement planning must be built on a solid foundation of protections. Another analogy I like to use to convey this concept is the game of golf. If I were able to send you to play golf at the next Master's tournament in Augusta, Georgia, and I could give you the golf *clubs* of any player who has ever played the game **or** I could give you the golf *swing* ability of any player who has ever played the game....which one would you want?

You would want the swing of course!

I believe that it is the same with financial products. You can buy most any financial product available through product salesmen. Likewise, you can go out and buy a cheap set of clubs from your local Wal-Mart.

Proper financial planning for a professional such as yourself demands being 'fitted for clubs' at the 'pro shop.' In other words, you need specific financial *strategies* from an expert in planning for professionals, and hopefully one that understands the veterinary world as well. Of course you can buy financial products 'off the rack' and piece them together from different discount providers (Disability insurance, investment products, retirement products, life insurance, etc.) or you can develop strategies specific to your profession and your desires. In this book I am going to help you with that process.

Having a solid financial *process* is more important than picking the perfect 'clubs' – i.e. perfect investments.

The goal of this book is not to tell you specifically which clubs that you should buy and it is not my intention to tell you *where* you should buy your financial clubs. My goal is to help you identify and implement a simple financial process that will pour the foundation to your financial house, laying the groundwork to comfortably live within your means. The overwhelming majority of financial advice books are written to tell the reader *what* to think. I believe that it is more important to help the reader with *how* to think. In this book we are going to discuss concepts that will help you develop your own financial philosophy.

Most of us go through high school and are offered one course in how to relate to money. Usually this is a Personal Finance course as an elective in our junior or senior year. The instructor will discuss general topics such as balancing your checkbook or how to open a checking or savings account.

If you are fortunate enough to go to college, you are again most likely offered only one course in how to handle and relate to money. It too is a general finance course that covers basic information but teaches very little real world applicable information. Often students take this elective assuming an easy grade and a reprieve from their serious studies. It is my experience that a person will have to go to the 'school of hard knocks' to learn what mistakes to avoid. Unfortunately, a person makes many of the common financial mistakes early in their life, and in a lot of instances they are never able to recover financially. Years later they are unable to identify what exactly happened and unable or unwilling to share it with the next generation.

Further, as I said earlier, I have found that young adults want the opinion of their elders- only when asked- and almost never want actual advice. Many parents and loved ones desire to share their experiences with the younger generation but are ill equipped to give specific financial advice beyond their own personal experiences.

Tragically, many of the common financial mistakes that people make have consequences that are not obvious and do not reveal themselves immediately. These decisions steal a person's ability to create wealth without them even realizing it until it is too late!

One goal of this book is to help you with the *thought process* of how you relate to, and think, about money. In the early stages of a person's knowledge of money we are taught that there is a common path to follow when planning for retirement and trying to grow your wealth. In today's media-driven climate we have become blinded by advertising from financial institutions and retirement programs such as the ever-popular 401(k) and IRA, the hope of Social Security in retirement, and TV & radio personalities with all the answers. It is imperative that you actively plan your financial future!

Most people spend more time planning vacations throughout their lifetime than planning for their financial future.

Some people even spend more money on those vacations than they do investing in their retirement! Simply sticking money in a qualified plan and hoping it all works out is not a legitimate plan. You must actively pursue your planning.

There are numerous events in your financial life that will deteriorate your ability to create comfortable wealth.

What is this book *not* about?

This book is **not** about directly instructing you what specific stocks or other investments to invest in that may help you 'get rich.'

This book is **not** going to teach you how to step into the gray area and evade taxes.

It is **not** about cutting corners or teaching you how to tighten your belt and buy one gallon of milk instead of two.

Everyone's desires, needs and financial situation are different. There is not a 'one plan fits all' strategy to guarantee success.

Proper planning requires discipline and a detailed path to follow. Let's get you started on the right path.

Chapter 2

MANAGING YOUR EXPENSES –
WRITTEN BUDGET

Is your current standard of living *more important* than planning for your future?

There is a war raging inside of your home as we speak. This war has been going on around you and you may not even be aware of it. Confused as to what war I'm referring? It is the war between your current lifestyle and your future financial requirements!

'Current You' doesn't think much of **or** about 'Future You' but I can promise that as you get older, this war will become more and more apparent. You need a plan to deal with this war now but how do you even get started?

It starts with a commitment to discipline. Personal discipline is one of the most difficult things that you will ever try to master.

When discussing discipline in a person's finances, I like to use the analogy of that person wanting to lose a few pounds. You don't put on an extra 15 pounds all at once. Even the biggest Thanksgiving meal ever eaten doesn't put on major poundage immediately. You gain weight one bite at a time. It is the same for getting out of debt and controlling your expenses. Most people do not accumulate large amounts of debt immediately. They do it a few dollars at a time.

25

Managing your expenses with a written budget is the single most important thing you can do for your financial future.

To lose those unwanted pounds (reduce your debt) it will not only take great discipline but it will require a plan. To keep the weight off (remain out of debt) a person will need a way to manage their expenses- a financial diet, so to speak.

In 2009, I helped create a course called 'Preparing for Your Financial Future' at Auburn University College of Veterinary Medicine. Since August 2009, I help teach this course each semester. Over the years I have met one-on-one with hundreds of students at Auburn University College of Veterinary Medicine, as well as Tuskegee University School of Veterinary Medicine.

I will tell you the single most important thing that I share with each and every one of these students, and also every client that I meet with in my practice. No matter how much money you make annually, you **must** have a way to keep track of your monthly expenses. No one that I have ever met with is smart enough to keep track of each and every monthly expense in his or her head.

The single most important thing that I can convey to you is how critical a written budget is to the success of your financial plan.

I provide my clients and students with a very simple Excel spreadsheet written budget. You may download that form at www.ethandawe.com/budget. You can see a copy of this spreadsheet on page 31.

Before you are able to make any big financial decisions, you must have a strategy to manage your monthly expenses with a written budget and manage your cash flow.

My preference is for you to use a *handwritten* budget. I would not recommend using a budget on a smart phone, tablet or computer application. Writing your budget down will make the dollar figures far more real than it may feel by simply entering numbers on a computer screen. This written budget worksheet is a simple, one-page sheet to keep up with all of your debt, assets, income and monthly expenses.

As you look at the sheet, in the top right-hand corner is a box for all of your fixed debts. The box below the debt box is for all of your fixed assets. I do not expect these two columns to fluctuate up and down dramatically throughout the year.

The box on the bottom right-hand corner is for your income. I prefer that you put your gross income at the top and then the *after tax* monthly amount below. I generally deduct approximately 25% from your gross pay and divide by twelve months to arrive at your after tax monthly funds available.

The entire column on the left-hand side of the page is for your monthly expenses. I originally designed this sheet so that you can fold it in half and focus on the monthly expenses. I am most concerned about the monthly expenses column. You should think of this column as a paper **monster** that will destroy your life if you allow it to get out of hand. It demands to be fed every single month. The only thing that it eats is *after tax dollars*. The moment that you cannot feed it the full amount it demands – It will eat *you*.

27

I would encourage you to print several of these blank budget worksheets. You should set an appointment time with your spouse, (if you have a spouse, I strongly encourage you to make all financial decisions together), turn off all electronics, put the kids and pets away, eliminate all distractions and go to work on filling out each monthly expense that you have.

If you pay for some expenses, such as auto insurance, on a 6-month or 12-month basis, simply divide the expense by the number of months you are paying and put that expense in the appropriate box.

It is imperative that we list these expenses accurately. Once you are confident that you have all of your expenses on your budget sheet, I would like for you to go back and put them on one clean budget worksheet.

One of the key features about my written budget worksheet is the small box just to the left of each monthly expense. This box is used for 'ranking' your monthly expenses. What I mean by 'ranking' is that I want you to go through you expenses and number them from #1 down based on what is the most important expense that you cannot live without. For my family that #1 expenditure is tithing. We believe strongly in the Law of the Harvest, i.e. you reap what you sow. For some people, they prefer to pay their car payment before their power bill, buy food or pay for a place to stay. I am unable to tell you what is or should be the most important to least important, but I can tell you that it is critical to rank them now. Why would you want to rank your expenses?

Unfortunately, at some point in your life you will- or may not- have enough money to pay all of your expenses for that month. Remember that this is a paper monster that will eat you when you cannot feed it. The only way to combat this potential problem in the future is to make more money or reduce your expenses.

While you are thinking clearly and not under the strain of financial hardship, I want you to make the tough decision of what bill(s) will not get paid for that month.

Every monthly expense that you have will be on this worksheet. I encourage you to put a lot of thought into what your monthly food bill actually is. I want you to think of how often you actually eat out instead of eating at home.

If this is your first time to do a written budget, I encourage you to empty out an old shoebox and place it on your breakfast table. For the next 90 days I want you (and your spouse, if applicable) to collect a receipt for **every** purchase that you make during those 90 days. Every single receipt goes in the box. I go so far as to make sure I get a receipt from the parking meter downtown when my wife and I collect our receipts. At the end of 90 days I want you to spread out every receipt and go through exactly where you are spending your money. I can promise you that this exercise will have shocking results- like revealing how much you eat out!

I would also encourage you to give quite a bit of thought to how much you spend on 'miscellaneous' and 'entertainment' each month. These monthly expenses are critical to understand exactly how much money you're spending on a month-to-month basis. It has been my experience that it will take several months for a person to know what their actual monthly expenses are within a $100 margin of error. It is imperative that you understand exactly how much money you have going out each month.

Before you buy a home, choose a student loan repayment option, before you invest, before you create a savings account, before you do *anything else* **– you must have an accurate written monthly expense sheet.**

Over the years I have seen the monthly expenses sheet of hundreds of people from all ages and all walks of life. What I have found to be true is that no matter how much money you make, you **must** have a way to keep up with your written expenses. If not, you *will* spend more than you make.

FINANCIAL PRESCRIPTION

To varying degrees of severity, I believe that everyone I come in contact with has 'Financial Cancer' and I know the cure!

To remedy this serious condition, I would like to write you a financial prescription. This would be similar to you going to a doctor and being prescribed medicine for your illness.

Your financial prescription to help you get better will be:

Prepare a written budget and divide the after-tax dollars as follows –

10% Giving

20% Saving

70% Budgeting (*not spending*)

10% GIVING

Regardless of how much income, or how little income you make, the principle of giving works. I believe that you should be giving 10%. If you are in a church, this of course is called tithing. If not in a church, I still encourage you to give.

Quite often I will hear someone say "we just can't afford to tithe or give." I believe that it's all a matter of perspective. Giving has to be a priority in your life. I also believe that the most valuable asset that you can give to another human being is *your time*. I strongly encourage you to be a giver of money, but also a giver of your time.

Regardless of whether you are a non-believer, a Believer in Christ, or a believer in another religion, the principle of giving works- GIVE!

20% SAVING

The second part of your financial prescription is 20% savings. I believe that you must be a giver and you also must be a saver.

I work hard for what I earn and I think that I should be paid for my effort. I often say that 'future you' is depending on 'current you' for his or her well-being.

Much like with the principle of giving, the 20% savings has to be something that you're dedicated and devoted to. We will talk more about where to put 20% later in this book.

70% BUDGETING

The third piece of your financial prescription is 70% budgeting. Most people would like to call this category 'spending'. I want you to get in the habit of calling it what we *desire* it to be. I desire to budget what I earn- *not* spend what I don't have.

Out of your 100% total budget is first 10% giving, second 20% savings, and everything else is the 70% that we will budget out all of our expenses. This will include all of our living expenses that will fund our standard of living.

questions? ethan@ethandawe.com

PERSONAL BUDGET

MONTHLY EXPENSES		
TOTAL EXPENSES		

DEBT	
Home	
Student Loan	
Auto	
Credit Card	
Credit Card	
TOTAL DEBT	

ASSETS	
Home	
Auto	
TOTAL ASSETS	

INCOME	
Annual Income *	
Salary - Pre-tax	
Other Income	
TOTAL INCOME	

| TOTAL INCOME - TOTAL EXPENSES = | |

| NET WORTH = ASSETS - DEBT | |

YOU CANNOT SPEND MORE THAN YOU MAKE!

33

Chapter 3

MANAGING YOUR CASH FLOW-
THE 3 ACCOUNTS

In the last chapter I discussed managing your monthly expenses. Now that you know what your monthly expenses are, you are ready to manage cash flow.

The first part of managing your cash flow is to consolidate all of your cash into an imaginary bucket. You can see a visual of this on the chart on page 39. All of your money that you have in savings, checking accounts or hidden under the mattress, should start in this imaginary bucket. Often when explaining this strategy I get asked what to do with an inheritance, a bonus from work or proceeds from the sale of an asset. Everything that is liquid cash that you can hold in your hand goes into this bucket.

Also note that we still have not decided how to invest, pay for a new car or pay off our student loans. There simply is no way to make any of those big decisions from an educated position without managing your expenses with a written budget and managing your cash flow with this simple process.

We are going to establish some rules for your cash flow. It is important for you to tell your dollars exactly where to go each month using the rules that you've put into place. We are going to refer to the first account that you are going to set up as your Operating Account.

THE 1ST ACCOUNT:

OPERATING ACCOUNT

RULE ONE

This is a basic *free* checking account. I bet you have this set up already. This is the account that will receive all of your direct deposit paychecks, as well as all of your liquid cash as you get started. Each time you receive a paycheck it will be deposited into this account.

RULE TWO

Your Operating Account will also be the account from which you will pay all of your regular bills. Each month the balance of this account will fluctuate up and down as you make deposits and pay bills.

RULE THREE

If you're still in school, or early on in your career, I would like to establish a new "zero" balance at $250. Once you are a gainfully employed veterinarian, we will change the new "zero" balance to be $1000. So what do I mean by zero balance? Currently, $0.00 is the bottom amount on your checking account balance. When you write a check for $1.00 more than you have in your account, you most likely pay a fee to the bank and potentially a fee to the retailer that you wrote the check to. As a professional you cannot afford to bounce checks all over your area, or overdraft due to too many debit card purchases. It's just a bad use of your funds to pay fees that are unnecessary. Eliminate this potential wealth transfer by keeping a safe, minimum balance in your account. Almost all banks offer an option to alert you when your balance moves below a specified amount.

RULE FOUR

With these strategies in place we will not obsess over our money. I like money. I like to hold it. I like to look at it. I like to spend it. I like money, but money does not rule my life. With this strategy, we are telling our dollars exactly where to go each month. The fourth rule places limitations on how *little* money or how *much* money should ever be in this account. Rule Four is that there should never be *less* than one month's living expenses in this account at any given time. Also, there should never be any *more* than three months living expenses in this account at any given time.

About every 3 to 4 weeks you should go online and check the balance of this operating account. When you have less than your specified amount you'll need to deposit more money, make more money or transfer money from another account that we will establish later. If you check your balance and have more money in this operating account than your specified maximum, then you will follow the next rule.

RULE FIVE

Let's say that your monthly expenses according to your written budget are $3000. We've established that your new "zero" is $1000. Therefore, if the maximum allowed under our rules in this account is three months living expenses, plus our new zero of $1,000. This means our maximum balance in this account would be $10,000. $3,000 per month expenses x 3 months = $9,000 + $1,000 minimum balance = $10,000.

Now before I lose you, and you panic about how much $10,000 sounds for one checking account, I would like for you to consider that what we are establishing are some very specific rules to follow. At this point in your career you *need* some very structured rules.

Let's say that you check your balance and you have $12,500 in your account. Rule Five says that you are to transfer everything over your three months living expenses and place it into the second account.

THE 2ND ACCOUNT:

EMERGENCY FUND

RULE SIX

The Second Account is a basic *free - savings* account in the same bank as your Operating Account. If you are still in school or early in your career, I would like for you to have 90 days net living expenses in this account at all times. Once you are gainfully employed as a veterinarian I would like for you to consider having as much as six months living expenses in this account.

Now again, before I lose you with how much money would be sitting in one savings account, I would like for you to consider that we're talking about setting some parameters - rules – for telling your money where to go. As you mature in your career, and if you were doing proper financial planning, we would place this money in some type of investment instead of just a savings account. For the time being, let's just assume that we're going to fill these first two accounts as I have described above.

Please keep in mind that this is an *emergency* account. It is not a new car, new pair shoes or 'I need a vacation' account.

Once this account is 'full', and all of our rules have been met to this point, we 'put a lid' on this account and move on to the third account.

THE 3RD ACCOUNT:

PLAN B INVESTMENT ACCOUNT

RULE SEVEN

Once the first two accounts are full you are almost ready to start making some of the bigger decisions that you are facing.

The Third Account should be a basic *free - checking* account in the same bank as the first two accounts. Rule seven says that once the first two accounts are full, and now when there is more than our specified amount in the first account, we transfer that money into the third account.

The *only* reason for money to come out of this account is to grow your wealth! Once this account reaches an 'uncomfortable' amount, and money is flowing into it regularly, you are ready to start making some of those bigger decisions such as:

- o **Can I buy a house?**
- o **How much house can I buy?**
- o **How should I pay my student loan off?**
- o **How do I invest for retirement?**

If you will use the written budget, follow the rules and manage your cash flow with this three-account system, almost all of your major financial decisions will fall into place for you.

It is imperative that you complete these two processes, in order, before you ever start: investing, buying a house, buying a new car, and paying extra on debt (including student loans).

This is foundational planning which works in much the same way as you would build a house. You wouldn't have the contractor go to your home site and start putting up walls and a roof. You would expect them to survey the ground, level the site, square up batter boards, have the concrete poured and allow it time to cure. In this foundational financial strategy, we have the same principle. You are going to patiently lay a solid foundation for your financial home to be built upon.

The Three Accounts Strategy

Managing Your Cash Flow

o All Income
o Bonus
o Inheritance
o Sale of an Asset

$

$

$

OPERATING ACCOUNT

o Zero Balance = $250 (student)
o Zero Balance = $1,000 (employed)
o 1 to 3 months Net Living Expenses
o Check balance every 30 – 45 days
o Excess $ over 3 months living expenses 'spills over' into next account
o Married – No Separate Accounts

EMERGENCY FUND SAVINGS ACCOUNT

o Basic Free Savings Account
o 90 Days Net Living Expenses (student)
o 6+ Months Net Living Expenses (employed)
o Once this account is 'full' – Excess 'spills over' into next account
o This is an Emergency Account. Not a new car, new shoes, I need a vacation account

PLAN B ACCOUNT

o The ONLY reason for money to come out of this account is to grow your wealth
o Once this account reaches an uncomfortable amount and money is flowing into it regularly – you need to develop an investment strategy that will incorporate the Velocity of Money effect.

CHAPTER 4

STUDENT LOANS

As I have said many times already in this book, I have met one-on-one with hundreds of veterinary students over the last several years. Without a doubt the most common question that I get from students is:

How do I pay off my student loan?

Almost everyone that I meet with for the first time says, "I just want to pay my student loan debt off as quickly as possible."

Please consider for the moment suspending what you believe to be the right way to pay off debt. As I said earlier, you go through life with your 'box of knowledge'. When you meet someone that has new information for you, and possibly information that is contradictory to what you currently believe to be true, you have the option of discarding this new knowledge **or** getting a bigger box. *Now is when you may want to go out and get a bigger box for a new concept that may be contrary to what you believe to be true!*

What I have done over the years in student meetings is help the student understand what options are available to pay off their loans. I try to explain both the pros and cons of choosing each option. If possible, I'll try to help them eliminate options that are unrealistic.

The first question that I usually get regarding repaying student loans is:

Should I consolidate?

My answer is: Probably.

A year or so ago, I attended a very long webinar on consolidating student loans, which was given by the Department of Education. One of my biggest takeaways from that experience was that it appears the loan servicers will strongly encourage you to consolidate your loans.

If you have loans *before* October 1, 2007 – and you choose to consolidate your loans- I *strongly* encourage you to consolidate the loans *prior to* October 1, 2007 *separate* from the ones *after* October 1, 2007. This allows you to choose PAYE for the loans you have consolidated that were taken *after* October 1, 2007.

In most instances that I have seen, I do not believe that it will harm you greatly to consolidate your loans. It will definitely make them easier to manage. Please note that this is not blanket advice, and if you are unsure what is best, you should seek wise counsel on how best to proceed for your personal situation. After hearing a depressing presentation from the Department of Education on student loan repayment options in the winter of 2013, I decided that there had to be a better alternative for students with advanced degree student loan debt. I spent almost 6 months creating a strategy that I believe to be the best repayment option available for those students who are carrying significant student loan debt.

You have six months from graduation to choose a loan repayment plan. In Chapter 9 I give you a 'To Do' list and I address the timing of when I recommend getting serious about this decision. I fully anticipate the laws that govern student loan repayment to change in the very near future. As of the first edition publishing of this book in the summer of 2016, you have the following five options to repay your loans:

10-YEAR REPAYMENT PLAN

This option amortizes your debt over 10 years. It is my contention that when your debt reaches approximately $100,000, the 10-year payment of around $1,300 per month is unaffordable.

25-YEAR REPAYMENT PLAN

This option amortizes your debt over 25 years. It is my contention that when your debt reaches approximately $140,000, the 25-year payment of around $1,100 per month is unaffordable. Of course, maybe $1,100 per month is affordable but I argue that it would severely diminish your standard of living… for 25 years.

INCOME CONTINGENT REPAYMENT – ICR

Nope.

INCOME BASED REPAYMENT PLAN – IBR

You must apply and qualify for IBR *each and every year*. Your payment is recalculated each year and is based on 15% of your last year's *discretionary* income. (See confusing government explanation of discretionary income on page 45)

At the end of 25 years your loans and interest accrued are completely forgiven **BUT** the remaining loan balance that is forgiven becomes *taxable as earned income* for the year that it is forgiven.

REVISED PAY AS YOU EARN – Re-PAYE

You must apply and qualify for Re-PAYE *each and every year*. Your payment is recalculated each year and is based on 10% of your last year's *discretionary* income. (See confusing government explanation of discretionary income on page 45)

At the end of 25 years your loans are completely forgiven **BUT** the remaining loan balance that is forgiven becomes *taxable as earned income* for the year that it is forgiven.

PAY AS YOU EARN - PAYE

My 'favorite' of all the repayment options is Pay As You Earn. You must apply and qualify for PAYE *each and every year*. Your payment is recalculated each year and is based on 10% of your last year's *discretionary* income. (See confusing government explanation of discretionary income on page 45)

At the end of 20 years your loans are completely forgiven **BUT** the remaining loan balance that is forgiven becomes *taxable as earned income* for the year that it is forgiven.

DISCRETIONARY INCOME

Discretionary income is defined as 150% of the poverty level in your state. Each state has a different poverty level according to the Department of Health and Human Resources. In addition, there is a minimum income designated as the poverty guideline for each household size. For example, a household of four people needs at least $23,050 per year to reach the average poverty guideline. So a family of four with 150% of the poverty level income would be $34,575 as shown in the following chart.

Persons in family/household	Poverty guideline	150%
1	$11,170	$16,755
2	15,130	22,695
3	19,090	28,635
4	23,050	34,575
5	27,010	40,515
6	30,970	46,455
7	34,930	52,395
8	38,890	58,335

Here is an example to help you calculate your discretionary income:

Adjusted Gross Income – 150% of Household Poverty Level

Sara graduated Veterinary school with $120,000 in student loan debt. She's now working as an associate earning $65,000. She filed her taxes as single and is the only person in her household. Her loan payments under standard 10-year term would be about $1,400 a month.

Sara's annual income is $65,000, which is a monthly gross income of $5,417.

The Poverty Level @ 150% = $16,755, a monthly amount of $1,396

- $5,417 − $1,396 = $4,021 discretionary monthly income

- IBR payment: 15% of discretionary income

- $4,021 discretionary income x .15 = $603.15 estimated monthly IBR payment

- PAYE payment: 10% of discretionary income

- $4,021 x .10 = $402.10 estimated monthly PAYE payment

Now you know what your options are to repay your student loans and you are asking:

What is best for me?

Below is a description of a strategy that I developed after the unfortunate presentation by the DOE representatives back in the winter of 2013. I call it:

Alternative Loan Repayment Concept – ALRC

(I figured I needed a snappy acronym like IBR or PAYE)

THE PROBLEM:

Many graduates from advanced degree education programs are leaving school with extremely high student loan debt.

Each of the 5 current loan repayment plan options result in a financial burden now (cash flow strain) **or** in the future (lump sum loan tax payment due).

THE OBJECTIVE:

Create a strategy that will address paying off student loan debt while allowing the debtor to:

1) Repay student loan in the *most efficient* manner possible in relation to: Taxes, Inflation, Penalties & Fees
2) Maintain a Reasonable Standard of Living
3) Retain Liquidity, Use & Control of Funds

THE SOLUTION:

Alternative Loan Repayment Concept - ALRC

Choose a repayment plan that will allow you to pay the *minimum monthly payment* for an extended amount of time while *strategically planning* for the potential, single year taxable event in the future.

SUMMARY:

1. Apply and qualify for IBR, Revised-PAYE or PAYE
2. Pay the minimum payment required, never paying 'extra' but instead depositing 'extra' into a safe investment described below.
3. Calculate year and amount of debt to be forgiven, allowing for potential tax rate change.

4.   Project amount of taxes that will be owed in the year loan is forgiven.

5.   Select a target amount of money to be saved.

6.   Choose a financial savings vehicle that is and/or has:

a.   **Historically Safe**- It *cannot* be subjected to traditional market risk

b.   **Reasonable Rate of Return**- Must at least keep up with inflation

c.   **Flexible to Rules Change**- If you do not owe some or all of the tax in the future, this investment should be tax and penalty free if you want to add it to your retirement.

d.   **Tax Favorable**- Must be accessible without tax and penalties when the student loan forgiveness tax comes due.

e.   **Collateralization Opportunity**- While you are funding this financial vehicle you need to have the ability to borrow money from it OR against it, depending on which is most financially beneficial to you at that time.

f.   **Disciplined payments**– Contribution to this investment must be routine and disciplined.

It is imperative that if you choose this concept as your repayment strategy that your investment meets **all** of the above criteria.

Please note that this strategy is *not* exclusive to my consulting company, Innovative Financial Solutions. I *do* have a specific financial investment strategy that I believe to be the *best option* to make this strategy work. I have successfully implemented this strategy for many veterinarians in the past and would be happy to discuss the opportunity to help you.

Why choose ALRC and how does it work?

It is important to understand and incorporate the advantages of current tax laws into the design and structure of your student loan repayment plan. Erosion caused by income taxes, and taxes on traditional investment earnings, has helped guide the design of the ALRC. I expect that laws will change in the coming years regarding how much of your student loan will be taxed and at what tax rate. Regardless of what changes may occur, our contention is that the most valuable dollars that you will ever possess are the ones you have today. Why?

Due to eroding factors that affect your money, such as inflation and taxes, the dollars you pay on your student loan are worth less and less as the years go by.

Our strategy is for the student loan holder to pay the minimum monthly payment required while strategically planning for the potential single year taxable event in the future.

- In the following scenario we will assume the student loan holder will choose the PAYE plan starting in 2017
- We assume they will owe the entire original principal student loan debt of $175,000 in 20 years – year 2037
- We will arbitrarily assume an income of $125,000 in the year 2037
- This brings the *gross* taxable income in 2037 to $300,000.
- Under the current tax law, a professional will have common tax deductions. In this scenario we will assume deductions of $100,000 for the taxable year of 2037.
- In the given scenario, the client has an Adjusted Gross Income, aka net taxable income, for 2037 of $200,000.

- If we assume a combined effective state and federal income tax of 50% in the year 2037, the client will potentially owe $100,000 in income taxes. (Note that your effective tax rate should be *significantly* less than 50%)

We contend that it is a more favorable position to potentially pay $100,000 in income taxes 20 years in the future than choose a payment plan that locks us into a high monthly payment for the next 10 to 25 years, in effect giving away dollars that are worth more today than they will be in the future. In our scenario, if the client simply saved $750.00 each month for 20 years at 0% interest, you would have $180,000. We also contend that with **proper planning** we can prepare for this potential taxable event in the future - *And pick up some additional benefits along the way with the same dollar spent. (i.e. Incorporating a Velocity of Money Theory utilized by banks, financial institutions and the proverbial 'rich people'.)*

COMMENTARY:

This strategy will require discipline. Under current laws, it is virtually impossible to be released from your student loan debt outside of debilitating injury or death. The student borrowed the money to receive a premium education with the high probability of earning a better-than-average wage.

The debt is real and the debt is owed. Under current laws, the client must choose one of the repayment plan options within six months of graduation or the loan servicer will choose the Standard 10 year repayment plan on their behalf. Utilizing the ALRC strategy, you can create a plan to pay off the debt as agreed but at the same time, and most importantly allow you to maintain control over the funds for as long as possible. With the proper financial product and proper plan structure, you can pick up many additional protections and benefits with this strategy.

Second to discipline, the key to this strategy is in selection of the proper investment vehicle.

The investment cannot be subjected to 'Elements of Risk' that traditional investments are exposed to. It must be liquid and accessible. It cannot be subjected to income taxes.

IMPORTANT NOTES:

- This *concept* is unique to Innovative Financial Solutions, LLC.
- The ability to implement this strategy is *not* proprietary to Innovative Financial Solutions, LLC.
- However, the key to the success of ALRC is choosing the proper financial product(s) while implementing the best strategy available based on your personal situation and future desires.

I have successfully designed what I believe to be the best strategy to accumulate dollars in a tax-advantaged manner, to meet the future loan repayment obligation. At the same time my strategy also includes, secondarily, solutions to manage other risks such as death or disability.

POTENTIAL CONCERNS WITH ALRC:

- You must file annual documentation and qualify _Each Year_ for the IBR, Revised PAYE and PAYE plans.
- This strategy requires DISCIPLINE. Each individual will have to self-assess if you possess the discipline to carry out this strategy.
- Changes in future laws. Please note: The investment product(s) of choice for Innovative Financial Solutions is structured up front to be flexible in the event of future changes in the laws governing student loans.
- All numbers in the given scenario are hypothetical. These numbers are intended as a reference to explain the _Concept_ of the proposed strategy **_not_** to give specific numbers and advice.

HOW DOES THIS AFFECT A MARRIED COUPLE?
Student Loans, Marriage and IBR/PAYE

I am guessing that when you decided to get married, it never crossed your mind on how it might change your tax status.

For those of you with student loans who are planning on getting married or are already married, it is important to think about your student loans. This is especially true for people on the Income Based Repayment plan or the Pay As You Earn plan.

What difference does it make? When you fill out the paperwork for your income based repayment plan one of the questions that it asks is if you are married. It is my understanding that if you file jointly, your lender will use both

54

of your incomes when they calculate discretionary income as described above. If you file separately, they will only factor in your individual income. This, of course, can make a huge difference in your IBR or PAYE payments.

Does that mean all married couples should file separately? Not necessarily. There are several potential influences that could be advantages or disadvantages to filing jointly instead of separately. There are no blanket answers when it comes to making financial decisions.

What about Public Service Loan Forgiveness?

If you do not get anything else out of this book, please hear this: All of these commercials and advertisements on loan forgiveness secrets are exactly what they sound like – Too good to be true!

There has been quite a bit of student debt discussion and legislation over the last few years. There are a variety of types of Student Loan Forgiveness plans offered by the Federal Government. A complete list of these programs can be found at http://www.finaid.org/loans/forgiveness.phtml

Public Service Loan Forgiveness:

If you participate in the IBR or PAYE, your loans can be forgiven after 10 years of public service. The government defines public service fairly broadly and includes all federal, state, and local government jobs as well as 501(c)(3) jobs (these are non-profit employers). It may also include you working in an under-served area of the country. If this is something that you are interested in perusing, I encourage you to contact your state VMA and inquire about areas that may qualify. An interesting note regarding this program is that the 10 years do not have to be consecutive, so if you work for the government for 3 years, work elsewhere, then come back to the government, you can still qualify after you've made 120 eligible payments (10 years worth). Having your public service payments certified could be an extremely difficult task. Keep good records and contact your loan servicer and make sure that you file all the necessary documentation with them.

The Federal Government's website on Public Service Loan Forgiveness is: https://studentaid.ed.gov/sa/repay-loans/forgiveness-cancellation/public-service

How you choose to repay your student loan will be one of the most important decisions in your financial life. I strongly encourage you to seek wise counsel on how best to proceed with this big decision.

Chapter 5

COVER LETTER & RÉSUMÉ
INTERVIEWING & CONTRACTS

Your fourth year of veterinary school will go by very fast-*Very, Very Fast.* I strongly encourage you to start the cover letter and résumé process early. If you are in your fourth year of school I would recommend you consider the following process to narrow down where you would like to work and target specific potential employers.

First, what part of the country do you want to work? Maybe the better question would be, is there a part of the country that you *have* to work in due to family or spouse commitments? Either way, I would like for you to consider narrowing down the area of your ideal home location and expand your search within a 45-minute drive.

Next, you will do an online search for all of the clinics within that area. Now get busy eliminating the ones where you have little interest in working. You can do this by checking word-of-mouth feedback with classmates and friends familiar with the area, as well as scope out their website and social media.

My desire is for you to narrow your list to the top five or six locations that seem promising. I would have you do an online 'street view drive by' of the clinic and immediate area. Now you are ready to rank them and target the top three. I want you to shape your cover letter to each clinic specifically.

It should be easy to discern who the primary owner of each clinic is and I would address your letter directly to them.

COVER LETTER

I would like to see your cover letter compliment the résumé. On the following pages, I have given an example of what I like to see in a cover letter, but I strongly encourage you to use it as a reference only and not verbatim copy it as your own.

o   Address them personally and briefly describe who you are and why you are contacting them.

o   Describe any and all experiences that may set you apart from other applicants. What makes you unique?

o   Wrap it up with a thank you and how you will follow up.

Always let them know that if you do not hear from them you will follow up, when you will follow up and how you intend to do so. The most important part of this process is actually following up in a timely manner. I prefer 7 to 10 business days.

When you do call, expect to be filtered by the seasoned receptionist. Part of the value to her employer is screening out annoying phone calls. Be persistent! Just because you don't get through the first couple calls, do not let this discourage you. There is nothing wrong with attempting 3 to 5 phone calls spread out over a few days.

SAMPLE:

Suzie V. Student

Anywhere, USA

251-555-1212

321 Main Street, Anywhere, USA 12345

SuzieVet@xmail.com

October 15, 201x

Dear Dr. X,

I would like to submit this letter and résumé for your consideration of employment as an Associate Veterinarian at your practice. My graduation date from USA University College of Veterinary Medicine will be May 10, 201x. I have a strong interest in working at a (small animal only/mixed) animal practice in (your desired region) and your practice fits all the criteria of a practice at which I would like to work.

My areas of professional interest include xxxxxx xxxxx, surgery, and xxxx xxxxx. I am eager to hone these skills with the support of your practice. I am excited to start my career and finding a practice with great mentorship is a high priority for me. I believe that my past experience, externships and carefully chosen electives have prepared me for providing high quality veterinary care.

In the past year, I have (experiences you have that may be unique to you)

I believe this unique education will bring significant value to your practice.

I understand that communication skills are a key to being a part of a successful veterinary practice. My strengths include being responsible, professional, with a willingness to learn, hard working, and a genuine compassion for both animals and their owners. I thoroughly enjoy working with and educating clients as well as appreciate the intensity of critical care cases, and value how they may help me grow professionally.

59

I would love to learn more about your practice and any opportunities available to potential new hires. My contact information is on the enclosed resume. I would appreciate the opportunity to follow up with you in a couple of weeks or hear from you before then of course. I am eager to visit with you and your staff to discuss employment opportunities in the near future. Thank you for your time and consideration, and I look forward to hearing from you.

Sincerely,

Suzie V. Student

RÉSUMÉ

Your résumé and cover letter should compliment each other. Items of emphasis in your cover letter should be on your résumé as well. I love the idea of a simple layout for your résumé, where your name and contact information are easily found in the heading. I really like a brief summary as the predominant top section. This section should be short statements of intention, value, and desire.

A section of personal highlights should follow your summary. A prospective employer will easily be able to tell what you are all about in a short glance of your résumé. Accomplishments and awards are a nice touch if you have accomplishments and awards that are noteworthy. I want this section to help show what you are interested in and what you are all about. Do you volunteer with a special organization? Have you received any special awards or acknowledgements? Let the prospective employer know in this section.

Education and Employment History are expected to be on a résumé. I have been asked in the past if it is good to put your GPA on your résumé. I am not a fan of listing your GPA, but it is a personal preference. I also get asked if you should go all the way back to working in a kennel as a young teen. Maybe. My hope is that you have really worked hard on the Summary and Highlights, and this section is more for letting them know who you are and what you are all about.

Always put references on your résumé. Never, ever list a reference without talking to that reference first, and not only get their approval but also know how they feel about you!

See my idea of a solid résumé outline below.

SAMPLE:

Suzie Vet Student

321 Main Street, Anywhere, USA 12345 | (251) 555-1212 | suzievet@xmail.com

---

Summary

Graduating Veterinarian dedicated to providing the optimum level of veterinary patient care and improvement of the veterinary clinical profession. Driven by sincere and genuine compassion for animals and animal owners, seeking to improve both the quality of life for the patients and the human-animal bond. Dedicated to _____. Strong interest in _____, _____, and _____. Personal qualities include _____, _____, and professional with concentration on providing empathy and respect to each individual.

Highlights

- Specific rotation that you excelled in or enjoyed
o One sentence description
- Specific veterinary experience that you excelled in or enjoyed
o One sentence description
- Specific rotation that you excelled in or enjoyed
o One sentence description
- Specific veterinary experience that you excelled in or enjoyed
o One sentence description

Accomplishments & Awards

_____

201X

_____

201X

_____

201X

Professional Affiliations

Student American Veterinary Medical Association August 2012- Present

American Association of _____   August 2012- Present

American Association of _____   August 2012- Present

Veterinary Business Medical Association   August 2013- Present

Education

Doctor of Veterinary Medicine   Expected: May 201X

Veterinary University; Anywhere, USA

Bachelor of Science: Graduation: June 201X

Veterinary University; Anywhere, USA

Employment History

Vet Love Veterinary Clinic   January - October 201X

- List of job duties
- .xxxxxx
- .xxxxxx
- .xxxxxx
- .xxxxxx
- .xxxxxx

Small Dog Vet Clinic   May 201X- January 201X

- xxxxxx
- xxxxxx
- xxxxxx
- xxxxxx

References

John Smith, DVM - Contact info

Mary Jones, DVM - Contact info

Mike Johnson, DVM - Contact info

Additional references upon request

INTERVIEWING

One of the most important things to me in writing this book is to help you interview with *confidence*. The only way to make sure that happens is to help you fully prepare for the interview by understanding your value. Some of the best veterinary-specific information that I have available to share with you is on interviewing, so let's get to it!

How should you dress for an interview? My preference is to dress 'business casual'. I would like for you to be able to 'scrub in' if the doc decides to sneak in a surgery while you talk.

If possible, get a two-day working interview. I often joke that these interviews are very much like a first date. On a first date, everyone is on his or her best behavior. If you can get that second date, you are far more likely to find out what it's really like to work at that clinic. You can hide 'crazy' for a day, but it is really hard to hide it for two!

When preparing for the interview I would like for you to have no less than a dozen questions ready for your interviewer. My preference is for you to have these written out on a notepad. Most of the questions that you want answers to should come up throughout the interview process. As they are addressed during the interview, you should mark them off in view of the interviewer to show that you have questions for them as well. Look for natural opportunities to work your questions into the conversation.

There are specific things that you need to know from your prospective employer to help in your decision process. It is my strong desire for you to almost be interviewing them back- in a professional way, of course. I want you to be deciding throughout the interview: Do I *want* to work here? How will it be working with this staff? What is the boss like when they are having a bad day?

The first thing you need to know is what do they expect your gross production to be for the first 12 months of employment. Gross production is the total amount of revenue or sales that you generate. If you add up your professional services charged, plus prescriptions filled, etc., that total amount is considered your gross production. The first question that you may consider asking is:

"Do you mind if I ask, am I replacing someone or am I a new hire?"

This establishes why they are looking to hire someone. One of the constants that I have found, not only in the veterinary industry but life in general, is that if you ask the right questions you can find out just about anything you want from a person. It is how you *phrase* those questions as to whether or not you get full answers. If you can get a prospective employer talking about their clinic, you can ask them just about anything you want. I have referenced this as being sort of like that scene with the bad guy and good guy in the animated movie *The Incredibles*. Mr. Incredible got Syndrome 'monologue-ing' and almost escaped. Seasoned veterinarians *love* to talk about their own practice philosophy and clinic. Look for opportunities to get them 'monologue-ing' and work in the questions you need answers to. If they are replacing a previous associate, your follow up question should be:

Do you mind if I ask what their gross production was for the last 12 months?

If you are a new hire, or if they seem reluctant to share that information with you, your follow up question should be:

Do you mind sharing with me what your expectations for my gross production will be for the first 12 months of my employment?

This is important to know because it helps you understand what your potential salary could or should be. It also may indicate what your potential for growth at this clinic could be.

The national average, base compensation for small animal-only associates is between 18% and 22% of your annual gross production. If they answer that the last associate produced $350,000 in gross production last year, and if you assume you can produce *at least* what they produced, you now know that your base salary should be somewhere in the $68,000 to $72,000 range. This base salary is *in addition to* basic benefits that should be provided by your employer. I will discuss what those basic benefits are later.

One great way to lead into questions that you would like answers to, that may be a little uncomfortable, is to ask questions that you already know the answer to in a confirming tone.

"So, how many full-time employed DVMs do you have on staff?" You may have already met three docs, but this question helps get the owner talking about their practice. Another great question is, "Do you have a practice manager?" Or if you have met their practice manager you could ask, "How is your practice manager used?" You are trying to understand how this clinic functions, who is running the day-to-day interactions, etc.

If the conversation is flowing well or you have an opportunity to slip it in, a great question would be, "Do you mind if I ask what the gross production of the clinic was last year?" This answer will give you a treasure trove of information! How so? Let's say they answer that the clinic did $1.6 million last year. Anyone who grew their business from the year before will be more than happy to follow up with offering to you that they were up 9% from the previous year. If they do not immediately offer that information, you may follow up with, "Oh, wow! Were you up from previous year?"

What else can we discern from this information? We know that they have three full time DVMs, plus the owner. We know that divides out to about $400,000 of gross production per full-time DVM. We may want to dig a little deeper with our questions to find out if the owner feels they had three full-time DVMs last year. Maybe they only work part time. We have to take into consideration that the clinic receives some of that $1.6 million of gross production due to sales generated from food sales, refills, boarding, grooming and other services that are not DVM related.

We would really like to be able to narrow down what we believe their actual gross production per DVM to be. We would have observed how many exam rooms they have and now how many full time DVMs are on staff. The average gross production per exam room is approximately $600,000 - $750,000 before it is bursting at the seams. The national average for individual gross production in small animal only clinics with gross production of more than $1,000,000 is between $550,000 and $650,000.

All of that information may tell you if there is potential for growth in relation to the facility. It may tell you if there is room for growth in relation to the current DVM staff. This should also give a really good idea of what they can afford to pay you, based on what they expect your annual gross production to be. By the time you are finished with this interview you may know as much- or more- about the clinic than the owner!

A key point that I do not want to neglect is this: Once you start working, I find it imperative that you keep up with your gross production. You *have to know* what your value is to that employer and potential future employers. All of the major practice software will easily keep up with production. If your employer does not keep up with production, you should keep up with it for yourself!

Back to interview questions. You may ask: What is the average transaction charge for your hospital as a whole? The national average is approximately $130.00 per transaction.

You may ask: What is the average transaction charge per DVM at this hospital? The national average is approximately $160.00 per transaction.

Both of these questions could help you decide if this clinic does not charge enough for their services, or if they may be discounting their service. Please keep in mind that if you take each of these questions and answers individually, you may not infer much about the clinic at all. The national averages that I am listing are just that – averages. I do not hold hard and fast to these averages for every clinic that I observe, but they are great indicators of what you should generally expect.

All of these questions are designed to help you decide if this is where you belong as a young associate.

There is more to a job that just money, though. I want you to interview with confidence and I want you to be able to make the educated decision of 'Do I want to work here?'

I encourage you to have an area marked down on your note pad full of interview questions with the classic T diagram. On one side I would write YES ! ! ! And on the other side I would write GO AWAY ! ! !

Throughout the interview process I would make notes of what is a Yes and what says Go Away. If you get through all of your questions and spend some time in the clinic observing employee interaction, workflow, and clientele, you will know if this is the place for you.

Over the years I have developed my criteria for new associates in order of importance to them and their career.

1.   What is the opportunity for mentorship?

Every new associate understands deep down that they do not know how to practice medicine yet. A healthy amount of mentorship is needed.

You may also ask: How are your technicians used at this clinic? It would be a great help to know if the techs do 'tech work' and docs do 'doc work'. Of course, you are not above doing what it takes to bring value to the clinic, but a well-run clinic has well-defined duties.

You may ask: How often will my performance be evaluated? I would prefer that you are evaluated quarterly early on and semi-annually as a seasoned associate. It is good to get feedback on how you are progressing. Accountability is a key part of life and work. Another question would be: What specific things do you evaluate on? Understanding what your employer's expectations are can only make you more valuable to them.

2. What is the work environment like?

Interview Question: What happens when there is an HR (Human Resources) issue? How do you handle an associate addressing a concern with another employee?

How do you approach an associate that needs reprimanding? Do they scream and throw things or demean you in front of everyone? Do they ask you to their office or to lunch? These are important things to know up front.

Early in your career you need a great support staff around you. Knowing that your employer and their staff value you is an important commodity.

3. Do I want to live in the area?

You didn't go to 8 years of higher education to be in an area that you hate living in! For many of you, you have deferred some of life's pleasures for an education in the industry that you have always wanted to work. It is extremely important that you have a reasonable social life.

4. You should be compensated for your full value.

I want you to make as much money as the employer will pay you. I also want you to be provided all of the standard benefits that a professional should be afforded.

Maternity

I have been asked my opinion on discussing maternity with a prospective employer many times. I can tell you from conversations with several owners over the years, including many female owners, that they all say the same thing. Every one of them!

They know you are most likely interested in having kids at this stage of your life. Addressing it during an interview scares a prospective employer. "I love this young associate but it sounds like I will be paying for maternity leave in the first year." In my opinion, the laws will protect you from discrimination while you are pregnant. Asking about maternity leave during an interview can definitely throw up some red flags for your prospective employer.

Contracts and Compensation

In most instances, your base salary should be between 18% and 22% of your gross production. For large animal practices only, the rate is closer to 25%.

Standard benefits should be provided in most cases. I have looked at dozens of veterinary associate contracts in the last few years and the overwhelming majority offer the following, in addition to base pay:

71

o   PLIT
o   AVMA dues
o   State VMA dues
o   DEA license
o   7 – 10 vacation days
o   5 + sick personal days
o   2 paid CE days
o $750 - $2,000 for CE

Some employers may offer a monthly amount in the range of $100 - $250 for health insurance, in lieu of paying for it themselves. This benefit is usually added to your gross base pay and is taxed accordingly.

Very few single practice owners are offering a signing bonus. You may ask for a moving expense allowance upon signing your contract as part of the negotiations. I have seen these offers in the range of $750 to $5,000.

Some single practice owners will offer participation in a company sponsored IRA. They may even offer a match of 3% of what you put into the account. I will mention my thoughts on this in the next chapter on Investing.

To Summarize:

The national average base compensation for associates in small animal only practices is in the range of 18% to 22% of your annual gross production. If they answer that the last associate produced $350,000 in gross production last year, and if you assume you can produce at least what they produced, you now know that your base salary should be somewhere in the $68,000 to $72,000 range. This base salary is *in addition to* basic benefits that should be provided by your employer. I will discuss what those basic benefits are later. If an owner states that they can offer you $65,000 in base pay, you know that they expect you to produce around $325,000 in annual gross production to earn your base pay. ($65,000 / 20% = $325,000). $325,000 / 12 months = $27,083.33 in annual gross production to earn your base.

My preference is for you to receive a reasonable base pay, plus all of the listed basic benefits *and* a 20% production bonus.

This would be compensation based on your gross production over what is required to earn your base pay. In most instances you will be paid for the first prescription but not on refills. You may be paid a smaller percentage on food, toys and accessories.

It is important for you to understand the basic math in regards to your pay. You may be able to negotiate higher first year compensation, but with it comes an expectation from the owner for you to produce.

Potential Interviewing Questions and Other Important Items to Consider

• Observe: Workflow, possible personality conflicts, and management style.
• How will I be mentored during my first 6 months, possibly up through the first year?
• Are there any special training opportunities for me in my first year?
• Why are you hiring? Is this a secure position?

- Am I offered products and medicines for my own pets at cost or a discount?
  - How many DVMs are on staff?
  - Do you offer benefits such as:
    - o Health insurance
    - o Disability Insurance
    - o Life Insurance
    - o Malpractice Insurance
    - o IRA or 401(k) option
  - Do you offer a matching benefit?
  - How many exam rooms are utilized?
- How am I paid for emergency calls? (If there are emergency calls)
- How many vacation, sick, personal days are offered with my contract?
- Does the Practice pay for my PLIT, CE classes and DEA license?
  - Will I have my own DEA license?
  - Who manages the practice?
  - How are patients scheduled?
  - Do you take Walk-ins?
  - How are doctors scheduled for exams?
  - How are new associates scheduled for exams?
  - How are surgeries scheduled?
  - How are surgeries scheduled for new associates?
  - What is my work schedule?
  - How are technicians utilized?
  - Does everyone here work well with each other?
- Do you have plans to expand the practice in the future?
- What are your gross production expectations for me in the first and second year?

- What is the average transaction charge for the hospital as a whole?
- What is the average transaction charge per DVM?
- How often will my performance be evaluated?
- What criteria will my performance be evaluated on?
- Does the hospital ever run short on inventory?
- How are HR issues handled?
- Have you had a lot of turnover with associates or technicians?

If the contract is ambiguous or vague, then you will have to decide if it is in your best interest to let it remain vague, or if it is better to ask and have it written again to be specific.

If an offer to employ you were made - unless they pressed me hard to give them an answer or the offer is revoked – I would ask if they would be okay letting me:

- Talk it over with my significant other
- Pray about it over night
- Sleep on it
- Fill in the blank with what you would choose!

Pressure to make a decision immediately can be a red flag to something that you are unaware of, which might make this a less desirable job that it seems.

While on a working interview try and interact with as many employees as possible. Introduce yourself and ask questions about what they are responsible for, as well as be on the look out for non-verbal ques. I would review the area around the practice. Do some research of where you might live. Check on the cost of living that you can expect in that area.

Chapter 6

INVESTING & RETIREMENT PLANNING

If what you thought to be true, turned out not to be true – When would you want to know?

Quite a bit of what you are about to read in this chapter may seem counterintuitive, due to the fact that it is not what you have heard from sources that you trust and believe to be knowledgeable. I think we would be in agreement that a great number of people struggle to make ends meet and by no means would most people be considered wealthy. I have to assume that the overwhelming majority of people I speak with have received the same type of information from traditional sources.

Instead of attempting to tell you what to think in regards to investing, I would like to share with you what I believe to be the truth when it comes to the things that greatly affect your ability to grow wealth. I will stick with general concepts and withhold specific strategies that I offer clients.

Almost anyone can design a financial plan that will work under a perfect set of circumstances. My question for the last 10+ years has been, "Does traditional planning work in America today?" There are many questions that need to be addressed as you develop your financial planning. What if taxes go up? What if interest rates go up quickly? What if you become disabled? What if inflation increases at a rapid rate?

What if you are not allowed to access your money in a qualified retirement plan because the government has changed the rules on how you can access that money? What if your investment portfolio does not perform as well as is projected to perform, or the market has a major correction just a few years from retirement? What if you out live your savings? (That is a common and very scary scenario!)

Possibly the most overlooked point and obvious fallacy when it comes to traditional financial planning is the impossibility to maintain constant mathematical assumptions throughout a 25-year strategy. There are eroding factors of money that require you to view money as a commodity, just as you would a basket of oranges. The value of your dollars erodes over time due to inflation, tax rates, interest rates, investment returns and other factors. Every financial product has advantages and disadvantages. You must know and understand both.

I subscribe to the theory that I first heard from Bob Castiglione, and reinforced by Don Blanton, many years ago that says, "If you will spend more time trying to hold onto the money that you have already earned *instead* of spending so much time and effort trying to find investments that will yield a higher and higher rate of return, you will be much better off in the long run."

There is more to be said of finding ways to eliminate or greatly reduce factors that destroy our ability to create wealth – and it does not require you to take risk!

I am happy to reveal the 'secrets' of wealthy people. Wealthy people tell every dollar that they have pass through their hands *exactly* where to go by using a simple process similar to what I have laid out in chapters 2 and 3. While the majority of people spend more time planning vacations than planning their finances, wealthy people follow a simple plan. The best secret to being wealthy is that wealthy people do not spend more than they make each year! They create a lifestyle ceiling for themselves.

LIFESTYLE CEILING

This is a concept that does not fit well with our American Dream philosophy but one that we would be wise to consider. The basic idea is that you purposefully set a lifestyle ceiling early in life. This way you do not spend a lifetime chasing a financial position that can't be reached, or one that if reached, can't be sustained.

The reality is that there is always something bigger, better, nicer, prettier, newer, and more stylish than what we have today. It is also true that the more we make, there is always something that comes along and catches our eye.

An important part of this philosophy is to set a lifestyle ceiling today so it does not totally consume every dollar we make. Failing to set a lifestyle ceiling can keep us from putting money away to take care of our future lifestyle needs and desires.

The lifestyle ceiling we enjoy today will also fund the lifestyle we will enjoy in the future. It is easy to get caught up in the moment of today with little or no thought of tomorrow. There is a great deal of pressure to maintain a certain lifestyle today, which can easily keep our eyes off of what will be required down the road.

Like anything, prudence would suggest balance. It would make sense that we enjoy a lifestyle today that will also allow us to maintain that same standard of living provided by the financial discipline we have employed along the way. Part of my job is to help prudent people do what prudent people should do.

The absolute best advice that I can give you, above everything else that is in this book, is to follow the budget I have provided in Chapter 2 to manage your expenses. Next, follow the rules to the three accounts strategy that I laid out in Chapter 3 to manage your cash flow. These two strategies will simplify your financial life and help you maintain control over your finances.

PREPARING TO INVEST

There are two major financial influences that impact everyone's financial well-being: The government and financial institutions. It is easy to lose site of the fact that these two entities are *for-profit* organizations.

I have found that walking into almost any financial business is similar to walking into a casino. Their building is the nicest in town. Their landscaping is perfect. When you walk in, the temperature is spot on. The colors and layout have been selected to help focus your senses to make you feel welcome and secure. The vault is usually visible and you just feel good seeing that huge door protecting your money. Everyone is dressed in his or her best attire, hair in place and they smell terrific. And of course, they are there to help and serve you.

Financial institutions earn money by storing, lending and investing their customer's money. They employ experts to develop strategies to make their company more money. They create new products, services, fees, penalties, interest charges and other hidden expenses to extract your wealth. Generally speaking, most people have not been educated on how to handle complicated financial matters that will dramatically affect their financial future.

I am not saying that financial institutions are all bad and you should not use them. I am trying to convey that financial institutions have a clear advantage over their customers because they know how to use money to build wealth. You need help combating them to grow your wealth.

The impact that the government will have on your ability to create wealth is enormous. The rules and laws that affect your money continue to change on an annual basis. Currently, there are over 75,000 pages of the tax code. You are expected to know and abide by those laws the moment you become a gainfully employed veterinarian. The amount of taxes as a percentage of your income that you will pay each year is extremely high. Unfortunately, because the government has broken these payments up into different types of taxes, most people are unaware of just how high taxes are as a percentage of their income.

Financial institutions and the federal government have the ability to dramatically affect your financial future. They use accepted built-in tools such as fees, inflation, taxes, commissions, interest charges and many other factors that can reduce your personal wealth. How many financial tools or influences do you have in place to defend against these powerful entities?

I am here to tell you that there are tools and strategies available that are plainly written in the tax code which allow you to do battle with financial institutions and the government.

The Two Most Important Points to Investing

When it comes to investing the two most important things you need to know about the investment are:

1. What is your exit strategy to get your money out of the investment when you need it?

2. What are the taxes going to be on those dollars when you are ready to start taking them?

The most common retirement vehicle is some type of 'Qualified Plan'. Qualified plans are any tax-deferred investments such as a 401(k), 402(b), IRA, SEP, 529 etc.

Your employer may offer for you to participate in a company sponsored IRA or 401(k). There are many different ways for an employer to set something like this up for their employees, so I am going to speak about how these benefits work in general.

Usually after a short waiting period, your employer may offer you the opportunity to put money into a retirement account that they have set up. They also may offer to 'match' up to a certain percentage of what you contribute. Most often I see an employer offer up to a 3% match of what you contribute. This means that if you make $70,000 in base salary, and you elect to put in 3% of your salary, they will take 3% of your earned money from each pay check and put it into a retirement account. They will *also* 'match' what you put into the account – up to 3% each pay period. For the year, you would put $2,100 in and they will match it with a $2,100 contribution on your behalf. That is your money now, but it comes with some rules attached.

You may be asking, "Why would an employer do this for me?" One, they are allowed to deduct the amount they put into your retirement account from their own taxes. Two, they offer this benefit because they want you to stick around!

Why do people put money into these types of retirement accounts? Let me start by telling you that almost everyone you know participates in some type of *tax deferred* retirement account. When I meet with people to discuss becoming their financial consultant and ask why they chose to participate in a *tax deferred* retirement account, I usually get the same answers.

- It saves me from taxes
- I am going to retire in a lower tax bracket

Both of these statements are false!

It saves me from taxes.

Tax deferred retirement plans are promoted by financial institutions and advisors as a tax *savings* vehicle. Therefore, the overwhelming majority of the population believes they are saving taxes when they participate in these types of retirement plans. If you take nothing else away from this chapter please understand this: Rest assured, you are going to pay the taxes owed on these dollars at some point in the future. It may be during your retirement, or it may be that your heirs pay the taxes after you're gone, but *you will pay the tax on these dollars one day*. More on that shortly, but first let me address a question I can feel you asking:

I have been told all of my life that I need to 'max out'
my 401(k) contributions every year – Is that not true?

I do not believe that traditional financial planning works in today's economic environment. It has been my observation that nothing is what it seems when it comes to what is considered 'common knowledge' of financial information. I absolutely hate the commercial from ING with people walking around the streets of New York, or doing yard work, with 'their number'. It is impossible to calculate what a person's specific needs are in retirement – 25 or 30 years in advance. A good book on this concept is by Lee Eisenberg, The Number. There is so much bad information and misinformation out there, that it makes common sense decisions confusing and difficult.

The most important thing with investing is not about the rate of return, although rate of return is important. What do I mean by that?

Let's say the following circle represents all of your assets on the day you retire.

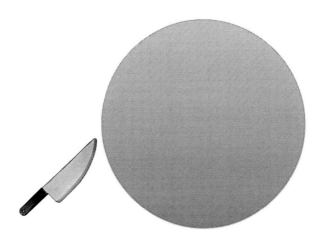

If I took a knife and made a cut from the center to the edge, handed you the knife and said, "Cut off the piece of this pie that you would want subject to taxation on the day you retire."….how big of a piece are you going to cut off?

Not very big! My guess is that you would take the knife and cut right down the same line where I made my cut. At worst there would be a few crumbs at the bottom to be subject to taxation.

So you agree with me – Rate of return is important but **the tax treatment of your retirement assets is far more important.**

Currently, almost everyone you know participates in some type of tax deferred retirement account, like the ones mentioned above: IRAs, 401(k)'s, 403(b)'s, 529 plans, SEPs, Simple IRAs, everything that you have ever heard of with investing, except for a Roth IRA.

When I speak to groups of doctors and the subject of investing comes up, I like to ask this question: " Think of the amount of money your last retirement account statement says you have…How much of that money is yours?" Invariably the entire room will tell me the same answer, "All of it!"

Hardly. Would you believe I have had *accountants* actually say the same thing!

These investments are *tax deferrals*.

You are <u>not</u> – 'Saving' taxes.

A more clear way to say it would be a tax *postponement*. I am guessing that not many people would be lining up for a Tax Postponement Retirement Plan if the federal government had come out with that investment vehicle. You are *absolutely* going to pay the tax on the funds that you are placing in these accounts. You receive a tax *reduction* today - but you *will* pay the tax eventually.

The question is, when you need that money what are the rules to get to it and what is the penalty? *Please note that the rules on how all qualified plans are designed and treated have changed every single year since they were created.* Every Year.

Once funds go into these accounts, you cannot take money out without paying the taxes owed for that year, **plus** a 10% penalty. After age 59½ they remove the penalty but you still pay the taxes owed when you withdraw funds. Upon reaching age 70½ they *make you* start taking money from this account. It is called a Required Minimum Distribution (RMD). They get tired of waiting for you to die and they force you to start paying taxes on that money.

Suffice it to say that I am not a fan of Qualified Plans as a retirement vehicle for most people, but certainly not for professionals such as you. You can do better!

The next most common answer I get when I ask why people participate in a qualified retirement plans is:

I am going to retire in a lower tax bracket.

Really? Your accountant today will tell you that you must participate in a 401(k) or IRA because of the 'tax savings'. They will say things like, "You will retire in a lower tax bracket." I would ask them, "How on earth will I do that?" Maybe an even better question would be, "Why would I *want* to do that?"

Do you aspire to make more money next year than you do this year? Of course! Do you hope to make as much money the year after you retire as you did the year before? Of course! *The myth that you will retire in a lower tax bracket is crazy to believe.*

Some financial planners will say, "You will not need as much money in retirement as you do while you are working." Really? Do you spend more money on vacation or while you are at work? Vacation. Retirement is a **permanent** vacation!

It drives me crazy to hear financial planners discuss their 'needs analysis' with clients. If you are anything like me, I do not want to 'guesstimate' how much money I will need in retirement and then *hope* I die before the money runs out! I mean, seriously – who wants to set up a plan where they have to hope they kick the bucket before the money is gone?

If you follow traditional planning, you will try to pay your house off as quickly as possible, max out your tax deferred account and chase a rate of return through your working years to maximize your retirement dollars.

The #1 financial guru radio host in America says that 'good growth stock mutual funds' have *averaged* 12% forever-that has to be true, right? I have noticed that he doesn't say much about how these investments will be taxed in the future though.

I believe almost anyone can show you how to accumulate dollars in an investment account. I argue that very few consultants/planners/advisors can do it in a tax efficient manner. Why does that matter?

Well, if rate of return is so important then let's say you are considering an investment with an investment broker and he promises you an average of 12%. Everything that you hear and read says that the market has averaged 12% since its inception. Naturally, you expect to be able to invest and earn a nice rate of return, and if the market has *averaged* 12% in 'good growth stock mutual funds' then it is not unrealistic to expect your 12%.

Prior to choosing a financial planner, you meet me and I make you the following offer: I can earn you a 20% *average* rate of return on any amount of money that you care to invest for two years – and *I Guarantee It*. How does that sound to you?

You are skeptical, of course, and so you decide to give me a test run for a couple of years and invest $1,000.

The first year I invest your $1,000 and I have a great year. I earn you 100% on your investment! You are telling all of your family and friends how awesome I am and are considering naming a kid after me. You now have $2,000 in your account and investing is easy.

The second year rolls around, I invest your $2,000 and unfortunately have a bad year. I lose 60%. Of course I had such a good year the first year that I tell you your money will definitely come back- but for today, how much is in your account? $800.00.

Are you happy with my results? Of course not! Did I do what I guaranteed though? Absolutely.

The *average* rate of return was a + 20%.

The *actual* rate of return was a – 20%.

Average versus Actual rate of return are two completely different measurements of your investment, and while both are factually accurate, one of them is the true indicator.

You will put money into a qualified plan because you think you are *saving* taxes. You will be told that you will retire in a lower tax bracket and you believe it because everyone says that is true. I can tell you from experience of working with professionals in all stages of life that it is a nauseating shock when you find out that the money inside your retirement account is not all yours. It is an even bigger shock when you realize that the government doesn't care how you earn income - actively or passively. They will tax an investment stream of income, such as rent from a house you own, or the payments from selling your practice in the future, or taking a little money per year from your qualified plan. They do not care how you acquire it – they are going to tax it as ordinary income!

There is a *great likelihood* that you will retire in a higher tax bracket than the one you start out in early in your career.

If you were to present this argument, your accountant or investment broker may then say something ridiculous like: "You aren't going to take it out all at once." **85% of qualified plans are surrendered in one check-** usually when the account holder passes away. A large portion of people *never* touch the majority of what they accumulate in their qualified plan, because their accountant in retirement will point out that they will get crushed in taxes if they choose to now withdraw money!

This brings Estate Taxes into play. There is a chance that, depending on how the laws change from today to when you pass away *(and they will change between now and then)* the money inside your qualified plan could be subject not only to *Income* tax but *Estate* taxes as well. WOW! There are states that have such high income and estate taxes that under a perfect storm your heirs could *owe* the government money back on the balance inside of your Qualified Plan.

So - how are your income taxes calculated each year?

Each time you receive a paycheck from your employer there are a few deductions that are taken before you 'get what you get'. City and county taxes are subtracted, as well as Social Security of 6.2% and Medicare of 1.45%. Then the state takes their cut of around 5%. (More in some states and less in others) And of course Uncle Sam gets his cut and that is usually around 20% - 25%.

Your employer is required by law to match your Social Security and Medicare. If you own your practice, then you are required to pay them both in the form of 'self employment' taxes. That rate is currently 15.3%.

As a side note: I absolutely hate when a practice owner puts it in a contract under the benefits or compensation section that they are paying your Social Security, Medicare and Workers' Compensation- as if they are doing you some huge favor. It is the law- they have to! This is not a benefit.

When you negotiate your contract with your employer and they agree to pay you a base salary of $72,000 – this is called your Gross Income. Gross Income is all of your income before deductions have been taken. Most people assume that you look up the current year's tax brackets, find where your income falls, multiply by that percentage and that is what you owe. This is not correct.

You are allowed to take certain deductions each year. You can choose a standard deduction or you can choose to itemize your deductions if they are more than the standard deduction allowed. You can deduct things like the interest you pay on your mortgage. I believe this to be a valuable tool in *legally* avoiding taxes. You can deduct charitable donations, medical expenses, and even student loan interest up to a certain point.

You are allowed to deduct up to $2,500 of the interest you pay each year from your income taxes – That is until you make $65,000 in gross income. At that mark the deduction is phased out, and if you earn more than $80,000 of gross income, you are not allowed to deduct any student loan interest. Congratulations - You are rich according to the Feds!

So let's say that you earn $72,000 and your total deductions add up to $22,000. We have a progressive tax scale here in the USA. The more you make, the higher your tax rate will be. After you subtract your deductions from your gross income you have what is referred to as Adjusted Gross Income. This is the amount that you will pay federal income tax on.

On page 91 is the 2015 Federal income tax brackets for a single filer. Keep in mind that there are different ways to file such as: Married filing jointly, Head of Household, Single, etc. Each of these options holds different rules, so we will stick with a single filer for our example.

Again, most people think that if their adjusted gross income is $50,000 - ($72,000 Gross Income - $22,000 Deductions = $50,000 AGI) - Then you just look down the chart below and see that $50,000 falls in the 25% tax bracket and you owe 25% of $50,000 or $12,500. That is not how it works.

It works like this:

You pay 10% tax on the amount of money in the first range: $0 - $9,225. = $922.50.

You pay 15% tax on the amount of money that falls in the next range: $9,225 – 37,450. = $4,233.75

You pay 25% tax on the amount of money that falls in the next range: $37,450 - $50,000. $50,000 being your adjusted gross income of course. = 3,137.25

Your total federal income tax would be $8,293.50. Of course you do not pay that all at once. Oh no. There would be mass revolt if everyone had to pay all of his or her income tax at one time. They take a little out of your paycheck each time you get paid.

To arrive at your Effective Tax Rate you would divide the amount you paid in income tax by your gross income. In this case - $8293.50 / $72,000 = 11.53%.

Rate	Single Filers
10%	$0 to $9,225
15%	$9,225 to $37,450
25%	$37,450 to $90,750
28%	$90,750 to $189,300
33%	$189,300 to $411,500
35%	$411,500 to $413,200
39.6%	$413,200+

I am often asked how to decide exactly how much your employer should withhold from each paycheck. My preference is the least amount possible. I do not want a tax refund each year. My ideal scenario would be for me to not owe them anything and them to not owe me anything. Why?

When people receive a tax refund they act like they have gotten something free from the government, when in reality all they did was get their own over-payment back.

In my world a tax refund is saying that the government took more money from me throughout the year than they should have taken, they kept it for an entire year, they paid me zero interest on what they took, and then reluctantly gave it back to me in a 'refund' check several weeks after I am forced to file my taxes and prove to them they took too much! No thank you.

What is your goal for retirement?

Most people's answer is something like this: "I want to pay my house off as quickly as possible and then start saving for retirement. I hope to earn the highest rate of return possible along the way, while taking as little risk as possible. I hope I save enough that I do not out live my savings."

My goal for my clients is to create as many retirement dollars as possible <u>that are unencumbered by taxes and eroding factors</u> and take advantage of Tax-Advantaged, Uninterrupted Compound Interest.

What do I mean by tax-advantaged, uninterrupted compound interest?

94

Let's say I offered you the opportunity to earn $57,598 of tax-free money over the next 28 days. All you have to do is hang out with me and be my pal for 28 days. At the end of those 28 days I will pay you $57,598 - **Tax-Free.**

OR

I will pay you one penny on day one, and I will double what you made the day before- every single day- for 28 days.

Day 1 = 1 penny

Day 2 = 2 pennies

Day 3 = 4 pennies

And so on... Which offer would you like to take?

Would you be surprised to know that on day 28 I would owe you $1,342,177.28? (See following chart)

Day (Year)	Amount
1	$0.01
2	$0.02
3	$0.04
4	$0.08
5	$0.16
6	$0.32
7	$0.64
8	$1.28
9	$2.56
10	$5.12
11	$10.24
12	$20.48
13	$40.96

14	$81.92
15	$163.84
16	$327.68
17	$655.36
18	$1,310.72
19	$2,621.44
20	$5,242.88
21	$10,485.76
22	$20,971.52
23	$41,943.04
24	$83,886.08
25	$167,772.16
26	$335,544.32
27	$671,088.64
28	**$1,342,177.28**

Most people find themselves in the position of holding debt throughout their life. In this position, a person goes into debt for a large purchase and then spends countless years paying on the debt- plus interest- only to find themselves back at zero where they started. They have never really improved their financial position.

A few disciplined people save up to make major purchases. They save up money for these purchases but when they finally do spend that money, they find themselves back at zero where they started. They *always* pay cash for *everything*, believing it to be the most favorable position. What they never take into consideration is the future interest earning potential they lose when the money is spent.

In the 'same penny doubled each day' scenario, if you saved for seven days (years) and doubled your penny, but drained the savings tank in the seventh day/year, your money wouldn't be worth much at the end of 28 days/years as seen in the chart below.

Day (Year)	Amount
1	$0.01
2	$0.02
3	$0.04
4	$0.08
5	$0.16
6	$0.32
7	$0.64
8	$0.01
9	$0.02
10	$0.04
11	$0.08
12	$0.16
13	$0.32
14	$0.64
15	$0.01
16	$0.02
17	$0.04
18	$0.08
19	$0.16
20	$0.32
21	$0.64
22	$0.01
23	$0.02
24	$0.04
25	$0.08
26	$0.16
27	$0.32
28	$0.64

The first penny example is a *perfect* example of tax-advantaged, uninterrupted compound interest and it is the only position from which you can create wealth. Unfortunately, very few people are able to enter the sweet spot of uninterrupted compound interest due to lack of knowledge. This goes back to my reference of getting a bigger box. What if there are strategies out there that you can take advantage of to acquire uninterrupted compound interest? As you begin to develop your investment philosophy, I strongly encourage you to take these concepts into the meeting with your financial consultant in the future.

Is compounding money in any investment *always* a good thing?

Would you be surprised if I said no? Well – Surprise!

Quite possibly the single most commonly propagated piece of investment misinformation around is that you are in the best position financially that you can be in- if you can allow your money to compound over time. Don't get me wrong; there are absolutely some advantages to compounding interest. But as I said earlier, there are both pros and cons to each investment and investment strategy. Almost no one ever discusses how compounding could have disadvantages.

The position where compounding does its most devastating damage is in a taxable or tax-deferred investment such as money market accounts, savings accounts, deferred annuities, mutual funds and tax-deferred investment accounts. (qualified plans) A very powerful marketing tool that is used by almost all financial institutions and consultants is a 'mountain chart' that shows how your money will steadily increase over time.

Notice that most of the growth happens at the later stages of compounding. In this scenario no withdrawals can be made to achieve the result shown. If the assumed interest rate is missed for any given year, the result must be altered from its original projection. The true effect of compounding must be over a long period of time.

What is not shown is the effect of taxes on compounding accounts.

Almost every financial advisor / planner / consultant neglects to take into account that while your investment is growing via the miracle of compounding – also the tax that will be owed at some point in the future is growing - like a giant I.O.U. to Uncle Sam.

In the chart on the next page I take the doubling penny example from before and incorporate a 30% tax rate to be paid at the end of each 'day/year'. This is a wonderful example of how taxes will devastate your ability to create wealth!

Day	Amount	Tax	After-Tax
1	$0.010	$0.003	$0.007
2	$0.014	$0.004	$0.010
3	$0.020	$0.006	$0.014
4	$0.027	$0.008	$0.019
5	$0.038	$0.012	$0.027
6	$0.054	$0.016	$0.038
7	$0.075	$0.023	$0.053
8	$0.105	$0.032	$0.074
9	$0.148	$0.044	$0.103
10	$0.207	$0.062	$0.145
11	$0.289	$0.087	$0.202
12	$0.405	$0.121	$0.283
13	$0.567	$0.170	$0.397
14	$0.794	$0.238	$0.556
15	$1.111	$0.333	$0.778
16	$1.556	$0.467	$1.089
17	$2.178	$0.653	$1.525
18	$3.049	$0.915	$2.134
19	$4.269	$1.281	$2.988
20	$5.976	$1.793	$4.183
21	$8.367	$2.510	$5.857
22	$11.714	$3.514	$8.199
23	$16.399	$4.920	$11.479
24	$22.959	$6.888	$16.071
25	$32.142	$9.643	$22.499
26	$44.999	$13.500	$31.499
27	$62.998	$18.899	$44.099
28	**$88.198**	**$26.459**	**$61.738**

There are a record number of people who call themselves financial professionals trying to position themselves as trusted advisors. Yet there is a record amount of personal debt, credit card debt and bankruptcies. At the writing of this chapter the federal government has acquired over $19,000,000,000,000.00 (trillion) in debt on our behalf- half of that in the first 231 years of this country's existence (1776 – 2007) and half in the last 8 years of this country's existence (2008 – 2016). Higher taxes are coming!

There are absolutely some advantages to investing in qualified plans. The deposits are tax deductible for that year, it creates retirement dollars, your earnings are tax deferred, you may receive a match from your employer and there is a possibility of borrowing from your qualified plan if you need money badly enough to pay the penalties.

I believe the disadvantages outweigh the advantages. You are deferring the taxes to a later date where you do not know what the rate will be. There is a strong possibility of those rates being higher than you owe today, early withdrawal penalty, possible loss of social security benefits if you earn too much in retirement, no collateral opportunity on the balance, complete government control over the account, expenses to maintain the account, penalties at age 70 ½ if you do not start withdrawing the funds, changes in laws that govern these accounts, potential for funds to be exposed to lawsuits, no deductions for losses within the accounts, potential for estate tax on top of income tax and the possibility of market loss.

I am certain that if you have made it this far into this chapter you are asking, "So what else is there?" I decided early on in the writing of this book that I would not use it as a solicitation tool for my consulting practice and instead use it as an educational tool. Therefore, I have withheld *specific* financial advice throughout. Suffice it to say, there are many strategies available to a proactive working professional.

Make certain that your financial consultant explains your exit strategy and the tax consequences on your future investments.

Chapter 7

LEGAL DOCUMENTS FOR PROFESSIONALS
AUTO, HOME, LIABILITY, HEALTH
DISABILITY & LIFE INSURANCE

There are certain protections that you need in place as well as professional legal documents. This chapter will discuss the documents and protections that I highly recommend to my clients.

Last Will and Testament

I strongly encourage you to have a current Last Will and Testament. When I say current, I mean that you should review your Will no less than every three years. For those of you who are married, you and your spouse each need a simple Will. Yes, even if one spouse is a stay at home parent, they still need a Will. For my single clients, I encourage them also to have a simple Will. Early on in your planning a simple 'I love you' Will is sufficient. An 'I love you' Will says that if I pass away, I love you and you can have everything I own. As you progress in acquiring assets, I would want you to have more advanced planning.

I would have you choose a young attorney in your area to prepare a Will, as long as you do not have significant assets. They need the business and you need to support your community.

Advance Healthcare Directive

An Advance Healthcare directive is a simple document of about five pages that tells your loved ones what you desire to happen with your healthcare if you are critically injured and unable to make healthcare decisions on your own. I have had the great misfortune of being part of the decision to withdraw care from family members who were unresponsive to medical treatment. It is *imperative* that you provide this document for the people that you care about so that you do not place them in a position to discuss what they *think* you would have wanted. Take care of this today! I encourage you to 'force' your loved ones to do the same for you.

Durable Power of Attorney

This is a simple document that allows your proxy to make basic financial decisions on your behalf if you are incapacitated. It does not allow them to sell your home and liquidate your bank account! When you are getting your Will drawn up, have your attorney prepare this document for you as well.

Auto & Home Insurance

I encourage my clients to shop their home and auto insurance every two years. I like my property-casualty (P & C) insurance agent, but I like my money too. It is prudent to shop around and see if there is comparable coverage for a cheaper rate. Keep in mind – *comparable coverage,* not simply cheaper coverage.

If you choose an agent who will not explain every facet of their coverage to you clearly, find a new agent. Insurance can be complicated. Please ask questions of your agent concerning what each term they use means. Contrary to what most people say, there *are* stupid questions. A lot of them. But you are the dummy if you do not ask a question that you do not know the answer to only to save some pride. You absolutely must understand what coverage you want and how much that coverage costs.

The first question to answer is: how much coverage do you need to protect your asset? If it is auto coverage, how much is the car worth? Does your lender require a specific amount of coverage? Probably. Same for your home as well – how much coverage do you need or does your lender require a specific amount?

If you rent a home or apartment you absolutely must have renters insurance!

The next question to answer is: what deductible can I afford? Your deductible is the amount of money you will be out of pocket if you have an accident. My thought on deductibles is to decide how much would I be willing to pay a paint and body guy to keep from having to file an accident with my insurance company. My usual answer is – All they will allow me. Meaning I would like the highest deductible available. This should also give me the lowest premium available as well.

Liability Insurance aka Umbrella Policy

I strongly encourage all of my clients to carry at least $1,000,000 in liability insurance. Liability insurance is also referred to as an 'Umbrella Policy' and can be purchased through your P & C insurance company. This is additional coverage that picks up where your liability limit ends on your home and auto coverage. 'Liability limit' means that there is a maximum amount that your insurance company is willing to be exposed to on your behalf for the premium that you pay each month. Liability insurance is generally very inexpensive and I would strongly encourage you to buy it.

Health Insurance

One of the many licenses that I maintain is a license to sell health insurance. I have never actually sold a health insurance policy, but I do keep up my CE to make certain that I can advise my clients on their options.

Health insurance…Wow, what a mess! Here is my thought process and what my experience has been since the 'Affordable Care Act' was passed in March of 2010.

In December of 2013 the premium for my family of five's health insurance from a major carrier was $364.00 per month. Our annual, family deductible was $2,500. In January of 2014 I received a notice that my health insurance premium would be $1,091.20 per month and the yearly family deductible would be $12,700.

I did the quick math and realized that I had to come out of pocket $25,794.40 before my carrier would pay anything and at that point they would only pay 80% on approved healthcare. When I did more math, I realized that even with a family of 5, I was being priced out of traditional health insurance.

After months of studying options I deemed the 4 major cost-sharing Co-Ops to be legitimate. When I do the math on what I am out-of-pocket with even the most affordable health insurance plans available - Even with the government subsidies offered through the healthcare exchanges - I am still ahead by choosing one of these options.

I chose Christian Healthcare Ministries. I encourage you to do your research if you decide to go this route. I found that CHM was the most reputable of the co-ops available. I would strongly encourage you read through the entire website and pay special attention to scenarios that are listed.

I chose the 'GOLD program' and added the 'Brother's Keeper'. What does that look like?

Gold program

$150 per unit, per month, with a maximum of 4 units per family.

The Gold program provides members with the ministry's most extensive financial support. It is my understanding that at the 'Gold' level, you have a $500 personal responsibility per unit, per year. Total bills incurred per medical incident must exceed $500.

Obtaining discounts on your bills may reduce or eliminate your $500 personal responsibility amount. You can receive assistance up to $125,000 per illness.

Example: You receive treatment early in the year for a gallbladder problem. Your bills total $7,500. CHM shares the total amount, less your personal responsibility ($7,000). In the middle of the same year you have some blood tests done (for an unrelated illness) that cost $400. CHM does not share these bills because the total cost of the incident is less than $500. At the end of the year, you break your arm and the treatment amounts to $2,500. CHM shares the entire amount of $2,500 because you have already paid your $500 personal responsibility in the beginning of the year. (This information was taken directly from the CHM website)

Gold program, plus Brother's Keeper

If you join at the Gold level, and also join Brother's Keeper, **you will have unlimited financial assistance** available to you for all eligible medical bills (after your personal responsibility is met)

My thought process was this: I can handle the common colds, broken bones, infections, etc. that come with life. I will negotiate with the hospital - with CHM's help - for as much of a discount as they would give to the insurance companies.

In the event that I have a significant health issue, I am completely confident that I will be taken care of by CHM. Since being members of CHM, my wife has been to the emergency room twice and had extensive blood work done. In each instance CHM performed exactly as expected and all bills were paid.

I have not had to make a claim for myself. I have ulcerative colitis and know that even if I must budget in the cost of a flare-up and semi annual check up, I am still significantly ahead in comparison to traditional health insurance.

CHM is **not** health insurance. I have found it to be very much in line with my faith *and* it is acceptable to the Federal government's mandate. I file IRS tax form 8965 each year and am in compliance with this mandate. For my family I have found that it is not only worth the money but it is the best alternative to the skyrocketing cost of traditional health insurance.

In the event that you do choose to use CHM - please consider signing up via our family's referral link at:

http://www.chministries.org/default.aspx?mem=172065

If you are interested in a Healthcare Sharing Co-op, but are of a different faith, there are other options available. I cannot speak to how each performs, as my experience has only been with CHM, so please do your due diligence before committing to a plan.

Disability Insurance

There are two ways to buy disability insurance:

1 – You can find an insurance agent that will quote you the cheapest rate on disability insurance available and hope that it covers what you would desire that it should cover. This includes buying group disability insurance.

2 – You can find an insurance agent who specializes in developing a contract that fits your specific needs and goals. This agent should not be 'captive' to, or promote only one company.

Disability insurance can be a very complicated financial product. You are a professional and it is imperative that you have proper disability insurance with a legitimate carrier.

Every disability insurance carrier has their own set of rules and definitions for what their basic policy covers. They also offer different 'riders' – additional coverage – that you can add to your base policy. Each company has their own definitions, and what their rider actually covers.

Over the years, there has been a significant amount of less than desirable information floating around the veterinary industry when it comes to disability insurance. If you are not completely certain of the veracity of your insurance agent, I strongly encourage you to ask the following of your chosen disability insurance agent and have them show you the answers in a *contract specimen*:

- What is your company's definition of 'disabled'?
- Who gets to decide if I am disabled?
- What does your base contract cover?
- What riders and options are available to add to the base contract?
- May I have a contract specimen? (A contract specimen is the company's base contract with caption boxes out beside each section, describing what is in that section in layman's terms.)

Keep in mind, in most states I can say just about anything that I want to tell about the disability contract I am recommending, *but what matters is what is in the contract that you sign and take delivery of.*

My preference for you as a professional is to purchase a reasonable monthly indemnity to age 65, 67 or 70, depending on what you desire for your coverage. The longer you choose coverage for, the more expensive the base policy will be.

I like a rider that is generally called 'Future Increase Option', which depending on the carrier, will allow you to increase your coverage with only income verification. I require all of my clients to choose the Residual Rider and explain the value of this choice.

There is generally an option of a 30, 90 and 180 day elimination period. An elimination period is the amount of time that you must wait after you are disabled to receive payments. My clients generally choose 180 days due to the planning that I put in place, which compliments their disability coverage. The longer waiting period you choose, the less expensive your base policy should be.

You should absolutely own your policy! First and foremost, if you own your policy you can take it with you to your next job without having to reapply for new coverage. New coverage will definitely be more expensive because you will be older. Another great reason is that if your employer pays for your policy with pre-tax dollars, and you receive a disability benefit from the insurance company, it will almost certainly be taxed as income. If you pay for it yourself with after tax dollars, as I recommend, it will come to you tax free in most cases.

I do not deem *group* disability insurance as the quality coverage acceptable for my clients. Ask your carrier if what you have is group disability insurance or if the contract you are buying is based on 'group coverage contract language'.

Disability insurance can be a very complicated financial product. You must get this purchase right!

Life Insurance

I love life insurance. Life insurance is the only financial product that you can purchase that guarantees what you *want* to happen, actually *will* happen.

I deem life insurance a *Want* product – not a *Need* product. Most people want to know how much life insurance they *need*. Typically what they really mean is what is the least they can buy for the cheapest amount.

If you are married you should have life insurance. If you have children you must have life insurance. If you are single, I still make the argument to my clients that you *want* life insurance. There are really only three types of life insurance from my perspective: Term, Universal/Variable and Whole Life/Permanent/Cash Value life insurance.

Term Insurance is exactly what it says: Insurance for a term. Generally speaking, companies offer 10, 15 and 20-year term insurance. Less that 2% of all term insurance policies sold ever pay out. *Less than 2%.* Early on in your career I believe that term insurance is a great protection product. I do not believe in the adage of 'Self-Insuring'. I believe that life insurance is a lifetime product.

Universal and Variable Life Insurance are life insurance contracts that have their performance tied to interest rates or the stock market. There is also a life product called Universal-Variable Life insurance, as well as a life product called Indexed Life insurance. From my perspective, I place these in the category of an attempt by the insurance industry to create insurance products that compete with traditional investments.

I do not like any of these life insurance products as viable options for the overwhelming majority of my clients. I do not include these options in the category of 'cash-value' life insurance or permanent life insurance policies.

Whole Life Insurance is also known as Permanent Life Insurance and Cash Value Life Insurance. Banks use this type of insurance as a cash holdings vehicle for their cash-on-hand requirements. It is referred to as BOLI - Bank Owned Life Insurance. Corporations use this type of life insurance as a powerful financial tool. It is referred to as COLI – Corporate Owned Life Insurance. If structured properly with the right carrier, this can be a powerful, asset-class contract addition to your portfolio.

No one wants to buy insurance of any kind. It is a necessary evil in most people's judgment, but insurance products are the foundation to proper planning for a professional. I strongly encourage you to select your insurance coverage carefully.

Chapter 8

SEARCHING FOR A HOME, MAKING AN OFFER & SELECTING A MORTGAGE

Let's get this out of the way first: Realtor is pronounced Real-Tor. Not Real-Uh-Tor. This drives me crazy!

Bad real estate decisions can lead to the biggest losses of your financial life. My wife and I have paid tens of thousands of dollars for the experiences that are in this chapter.

The average American family moves every seven years. My experience with buying homes has led me to realize I should not fall in love with a house. It's just a pile of bricks. When searching for a home, if the deal isn't a good one - walk away. There are plenty of other houses to buy. For those of you who are first time buyers, take advantage of the fact that you are not in a mind-numbing panic to find a place to live. Most house hunters have just sold their home and must find a home in a matter of days. Coordinating the "get out" date of the house you sold, with the first day available to "move into" the new house, can be extremely difficult and stressful.

When you are ready to start the home search process it is a really good idea to find an agent to represent you. This is called a 'buyer's agent'. Any of the real estate agents in the pamphlets can represent you. I would *never* call the name on the sign in front of a home you are interested in. They are the 'seller's agent' and represent the seller *first*, to sell the home at the highest price possible. Your buyer's agent will be paid well to show you homes in your desired area and within your price range. I would encourage you to see as many houses all over your new area as possible. Please do not get caught up in the made-for-television, house hunter type shows. There are many things that go on behind the scenes that are never shown and the agents almost always show the prospective buyer houses out of their price range.

Remember that if you have gone through the process of managing your expenses and managing your cash flow, as I described earlier, you will be able to determine how much you can afford to spend on your new home.

Before making an offer, consider riding through the neighborhood at different times of the day, night and weekends. This will help you get a feel for noise, kids and other potentially undesirable stuff that may drive you crazy once you move in. This will save you a headache later.

In the past I have asked my agents if they would check with neighbors for me and see what the neighborhood is like. I would rather make an uncomfortable request of my agent, who is making money off of my purchase, to find out if there is anything odd in the area.

You would be surprised what you can find out by asking the two neighbors beside your potential home and the three across the street. These are people that you will be connected to for many years to come. It would be nice to know a little about the neighborhood before buying a $200,000 investment!

Find out what the Home Owners Association is like in your chosen neighborhood **prior to making an offer**! Are they HOA crazies, or reasonable common sense folks? (I **hate** dealing with HOA.)

Check out the buzz regarding the local school district. Being in a desirable school district is important for potential resale.

Making an Offer

When you are ready to make an offer there are several things for you to consider. I would like for you to do your due diligence on how much it will cost you to repair all of the items that you bird-dogged when you first viewed the home. I would not hesitate to ask for a second, or even third showing, to make sure that you really like this home. Buying a house is a big decision!

If the first offer you make doesn't make you sort of giggle, it is most likely too high. Of course, you do not want to risk offending the seller but you *do* want the best deal you can get. If your real estate agent is not willing to make the initial offer you propose, then you might consider a new realtor.

As I have said before of other professionals - The real estate agent works for you. You want all the information that they can provide and maintain the same professional respect that you will desire in your exam room, but ultimately *you* have to pay for the home. Real estate commissions are **always** negotiable. Just because they say they charge 7% - 10% doesn't mean that is what they will accept.

If you make an offer on a home and the seller counters with an offer close to what you willing to pay, ask both the seller's agent and your buyer's agent if they will consider giving up some commission to close the gap.

Yes - Some of these type things may possibly make you

seem cheap and it potentially creates an awkward moment in conversation, but those who do not ask for discounts and commission breaks pay more money than those who do.

Is it worth a few minutes of awkward silence to save $10,000.00? Yes.

This all may seem like a lot of work or a hassle, but we are talking about making one of the biggest purchases you will ever make. This is a *huge* financial transaction and you need to do all the due diligence that you can to get the biggest bang for your buck. I have said that if the opening offer doesn't make you blush it is too high- but you can't just throw out a low ball number and say, "*Wham-* What do you think about this offer?" **You should be able to professionally justify a low offer.**

Once you zero in on a home that you want to make an offer on, have your agent pull comparables - 'comps' - on houses that have sold in the area recently. It is <u>very important</u> that you look over the detailed specifics of each comparable home sold. You should consider the age of home, square footage, lot size, pool or no pool, etc. I like to see 4, 5 or even 6 comps on homes as similar as possible to the one you are considering placing an offer on. These comps will give you a great idea of what your potential home **should** sell for.

Obviously, if the asking price on the home you are interested in is more than the recent comps, then that will be your major justification for your lower starting offer.

Next would be to see if there is anything about this particular home that may make it less desirable than the comps that were pulled. Does it fall into a different, less desirable school district? Are there any unsightly homes or businesses nearby? When you are viewing the home, I recommend you really check it out thoroughly. My wife and I will use the old 'bird dog' technique, where one of us will point out everything we can see that is wrong with the home. Does it need new flooring? Every house needs paint when someone moves out. Are the kitchens and baths outdated? How old is the roof and A/C unit? These are all items that you can negotiate out of the price of the home when you are ready to make an offer. It always helps to take someone with you that is close enough to you to tell you the truth, but not so close that they irritate you! They can help point out things that you are not going to see.

From my experience I strongly encourage you to **always** make your offer contingent on:

- An Acceptable Home Inspection
- Suitable Financing (Wording: "Offer contingent on buyer receiving suitable financing")
- Termite Bond (Seller will have to provide this at their expense)

Once you have made an offer and they accept, you and your agent will line up the Home Inspection. Remember, the offer is contingent on a *suitable* home inspection. No house built will be in perfect working order after a thorough home inspection. This contingency gives you an out even after you have made your offer to purchase, if you change your mind during the home inspection.

If at all possible you need to be there when the home inspector is inspecting the home. You should take a note pad and make notes of every little thing they identify as a possible issue, without getting in their way of course.

Ask the inspector if they have a ballpark of how much each repair will cost. These are all negotiable issues when you make your new offer. If the inspector cannot give you ballpark repair figures, it is easy to call around to plumbers, painters and a local contractor to get these figures. If the inspection report is not super clean, it is absolutely customary to make a new offer based on repairs that were identified during the inspection. They have the option of either repairing the issues to your satisfaction or reducing the price of the home. If you have done your due diligence, you should give them the ballpark repair figures based on your research, not just your opinion.

It is important to acknowledge that this is your first, starter home. You may have a purchase price number in mind already but consider that making a good purchase is important. Buying within your budget is critical to your financial future. If you buy too much house now it could come back to bite you in the future if things do not work out exactly as planned.

Use your budget worksheet and cash flow to see how much of a house you can afford and do not forget all the other things that it takes to run a household. Some examples are:

Garbage

Water

Power

Gas

Phone

Alarm

Insurance

HOA Dues

Property Taxes

Lawn Care

House Cleaner

Miscellaneous maintenance - Stuff will break. Some of that can get expensive!

Home Warranty

There is such a thing as a 'Home Warranty' that you can purchase, that will insure you against big expense items 'going bad' within a specified number of years. This might be worth looking into, especially if your home is a little older. Although it is not common for the seller to pay for a home warranty, it will not hurt to request that the seller pay for this protection.

There is a good chance that you will have to make a big purchase of a new fridge or washer and dryer. Also, do not forget that the cost of furnishing your new home can be a huge expense! Here is a lesson my wife and I have learned the hard way: Do not go out on a furniture hunt and buy everything you want or need in a weekend. Space it out over several weeks, or even months. Patiently wait for traditional deal days such as President's Day, 4th of July, Memorial Day, etc., or even shop local flea markets and consignment stores. This gives you a chance to pick furniture you want instead of just frantically going out and buying stuff.

There are tons of websites that give a lot of information on the homes in your market. In the past my wife has been able to look up a property and tell how long it has been on the market, how many times it has been listed, what the original asking price was, how many times the price has been lowered, what the taxes were last year and much more.

These are just several tips that I can offer to you based on many mistakes in my past when buying real estate. Buying a house is quite possibly the largest single purchase that you will make in your lifetime. It is imperative that you are diligent in your decision making process! I encourage you to seek wise counsel when you make your first home purchase.

Selecting a Mortgage

Choosing the right loan can be confusing because there is a lot of misinformation available to consumers when it comes to selecting a mortgage. If banks and mortgage companies made the same amount on each mortgage, how many options do you think would be offered? One. In fact, there are many options when it comes to choosing a mortgage.

In this section I will not attempt to tell you about all of the options, nor tell you what option you should choose. Instead, I would like to give you some basic information about mortgages and then introduce you to three couples that will give you a scenario of the extremes.

The three most common mortgage options are a 30-year fixed rate loan, a 15-year fixed rate loan and an Adjustable Rate Mortgage - ARM.

A **30 year fixed rate mortgage** amortizes your principal borrowed amount over 30 years at a fixed interest rate. For instance, if you bought a home for $160,000 with all the closing costs included, your lender may offer you a 5% interest rate for 30 years. Your lender can print an amortization schedule, which shows you when each payment is due, all of the basic terms of the loan, as well as show how much of each payment is principal and how much is interest. Early on in any loan the overwhelming majority of your payment will be interest. In later years you will pay more principal with each payment.

Generally the interest rate on a 30-year fixed rate mortgage is a little higher than a 15-year fixed rate mortgage.

An illustration of an amortization schedule (partial) for a 30-year fixed rate mortgage is shown below. (Screen shots taken from www.bankrate.com)

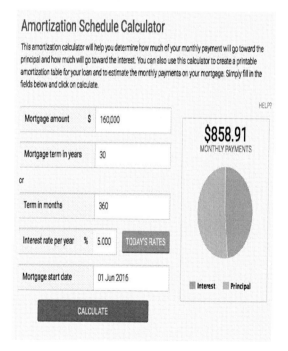

A **15 year fixed rate mortgage** amortizes your principal borrowed amount over 15 years, at a fixed interest rate. If we use the previous example of $160,000 at 5% interest you can see by the following chart the difference in the 30-year mortgage.

DATE	PAYMENT	PRINCIPAL	INTEREST	TOTAL INTEREST	BALANCE
July 2016	$858.91	$192.25	$666.67	$666.67	$159,807.75
Aug. 2016	$858.91	$193.05	$665.87	$1,332.53	$159,614.70
Sept. 2016	$858.91	$193.85	$665.06	$1,997.59	$159,420.85
Oct. 2016	$858.91	$194.66	$664.25	$2,661.85	$159,226.19
Nov. 2016	$858.91	$195.47	$663.44	$3,325.29	$159,030.72
Dec. 2016	$858.91	$196.29	$662.63	$3,987.92	$158,834.43
Jan. 2017	$858.91	$197.10	$661.81	$4,649.73	$158,637.33
Feb. 2017	$858.91	$197.93	$660.99	$5,310.72	$158,439.40
Mar. 2017	$858.91	$198.75	$660.16	$5,970.88	$158,240.65
April 2017	$858.91	$199.58	$659.34	$6,630.22	$158,041.07
May 2017	$858.91	$200.41	$658.50	$7,288.72	$157,840.66
June 2017	$858.91	$201.25	$657.67	$7,946.39	$157,639.42
July 2017	$858.91	$202.08	$656.83	$8,603.22	$157,437.33
Aug. 2017	$858.91	$202.93	$655.99	$9,259.21	$157,234.41
Sept. 2017	$858.91	$203.77	$655.14	$9,914.35	$157,030.63
Oct. 2017	$858.91	$204.62	$654.29	$10,568.65	$156,826.01
Nov. 2017	$858.91	$205.47	$653.44	$11,222.09	$156,620.54

On the surface it may seem that a 15-year mortgage is much better than a 30-year mortgage. It may appear that you can pay a 15-year mortgage off quicker than a 30-year mortgage, and save a lot of interest that you would otherwise pay in a 30-year mortgage. But are there many other factors to take into consideration that may affect your repayment strategy.

Remember earlier in this book I talked about those times in life when you meet someone with a different idea of how a common issue should be approached, or a new idea that you have never heard of. You get to decide if you reject this new information, if it will fit into your current box of knowledge, or if you need to get a bigger box to put this new information in. I am about to challenge what you think you know about paying off large debt, such as a home.

Instead of telling you what mortgage is best for you, I would like to offer a story of three couples that chose three completely different mortgage options. Don Blanton first introduced me to this illustration. He has an amazing ability to use simple, common sense stories to convey somewhat complex strategies.

Using his illustration as my guide, I will walk you through how each family's decision works out. At the end of the story it is my hope that you are able to choose the mortgage that is right for you instead of making a decision based on what 'feels' right.

The Pre-Story Quiz

True or False

• A large down payment will save you more money on your mortgage over time, than a small down payment.

• A 15-year mortgage will save you more money than a 30-year mortgage.

• Making extra principal payments saves you money over the life of your mortgage.

• The interest rate is the *main factor* in determining the cost of a mortgage.

- You are financially more secure having your home paid off, than having it financed 100%.

Most people only look at two factors when choosing a mortgage: payment amount and interest rate. There are several other factors to be considered in determining what mortgage is right for you. Inflation, tax deductions, down payments, liquidity-use-control of your money and opportunity costs all come into play.

In this story we are going to look at three families. They are all buying *identical* $300,000 homes. As we move through this story I would like for you to reflect back on the five true or false questions and consider which one of these families are in the best financial position at the end.

Our three families are:

The Free & Clears

The Owe It Alls

The Pay Extras

The Free & Clears have $300,000 in the bank and decided not to take out a mortgage. They have chosen to pay their house off with one check. They are 'free and clear' of all house debt and have no monthly mortgage payment. Their plan is to invest what their monthly payment would be into a safe tax-*deferred* investment.

The Owe It Alls have $300,000 in the bank but they decided to do 100% financing on their home. They chose a 30-year fixed rate mortgage. Their plan is to invest their $300,000 into a safe tax-*advantaged* investment.

The Pay Extras did not have enough money to buy a house like the two previous couples. You may find that you are very much like the 'Pay Extras' in this story. I have found over the years that most people find themselves in this position. Many of the 'financial guru' television and talk radio hosts prefer this position for their listeners.

The Pay Extras put the largest down payment that they can possibly afford and chose a 15-year mortgage. They decided that it was their best strategy to pay extra every opportunity that they can, and pay this home off as quickly as possible.

They are unable to participate in a tax-deferred retirement account because they are paying extra on their mortgage. They plan on investing everything they can afford *after* they pay their home off.

I wonder which one of these positions you find yourself gravitating toward. As I said earlier, there are many issues in addition to interest rate that are important to consider. One of those factors is called **inflation.**

The federal government calculates inflation for us each year but they do not include fuel and energy. When working with a traditional financial consultant, they will use 3% as the commonly accepted inflation rate. I believe that inflation is actually much higher than that, but for the purpose of this story let's assume that inflation is 3%. How will inflation affect each one of our couples?

Let's say The Owe It Alls have a 30-year fixed rate mortgage at 4% interest and their payment is $1500 dollars per month. What will that same $1500 buy in 10 years, 20 years or even 30 years?

If you use any inflationary calculator that's available online, and you put in 30 years at 3% inflation, $1500 will spend like $617.98, 30 years in the future. *Due to inflation, the payments that you make in the early years of a mortgage are your most valuable dollars.* There are actually other factors that will affect the value of a dollar over those years as well.

The Free & Clears gave their most valuable dollars away upfront and voluntarily. In fact, they gave away the most that they could have given by paying their home off with one check.

The Pay Extras gave up the maximum dollars that they had available upfront and voluntarily. They also give up dollars each month that are their most valuable dollars, by paying extra.

The Owe It Alls have a fixed mortgage with the minimum payment that the lender will allow. Over the 30 years of their loan, they will give their lender payments that are worth less and less, while investing to offset for inflation.

Most people make a large down payment to reduce their monthly payments and 'save interest'. But does their down payment *earn* them any interest? No, of course not. This is called **Lost Opportunity Cost.**

Lost Opportunity Cost is this: For every dollar you acquire, you may choose to spend or invest. Invested dollars grow overtime. Spent dollars are gone forever. Let's say you have $100, you invest it and earn 10%. You now have $110. Let's say you have another $100 and before you have the opportunity to invest it, you have to spend it- on food, interest on student loans or a car payment- any expense that you have to pay where you would have otherwise been able to keep and invest that $100. How much did that cost you? It cost you the $100 that you had to spend **but** it also cost you what the $100 could have earned, had you been able to keep and invest those dollars.

How does the size of each family's down payment affect their future? Each family had the opportunity to put a down payment on their home. We said that each family bought identical $300,000 houses.

The Free & Clears put the largest down payment possible on their home- all of it - $300,000.

The Pay Extras put down the most they could afford and are accelerating the payoff every chance they get by paying extra.

The Owe It Alls put zero down and pay only the minimum required monthly payment. As we said, they had $300,000 but chose to take out the mortgage and invest the full $300,000. Of course they now have a $1,500 per month mortgage to pay, but this allows them to give the lender payments that are worth less and less, while investing to offset inflation. And the interest portion of their monthly payments is tax deductible, which reduces their effective cost of borrowing. Assuming a rate of return of 6%, the $300,000 the Owe It Alls chose not to put down on their home, but chose to invest, will grow to **$1,723,047.35** over 30 years.

The $300,000 that the Free & Clears 'put down' on their home earns no interest **and** they give up their most valuable dollars. This is due to the deteriorating factors of money, namely inflation. Of course, they can now start investing with the dollars that they would have otherwise had to pay in monthly payments. They chose to give up control of their money to the lender, and they do not have the mortgage interest deduction. Therefore they will have to assume a higher risk than the Owe It Alls in their investment strategy.

I would say that if the Free & Clears cannot sell their house for $1,723,047.35 in 30 years, they might have made a *slight* financial error.

Money used for a down payment earns no interest, is controlled by the lender- not you- and reduces your tax deductions. Quite possibly the ideal amount to put down on a home could be zero, based strictly as a financial decision.

Some people say that their home is their number one investment, but is it a good investment? The average family moves every seven years. The early payments in a 15-year or 30-year mortgage are almost all interest. The first seven years of your payments are most certainly made up of a majority of interest, per payment.

Let's assume that 15 years in the future each of these family's homes are now worth $500,000. Not bad, huh? Remember they paid $300,000 15 years ago. Now let's say that the Free & Clears have spent $40,000 on this house in taxes, insurance, expenses, upkeep and miscellaneous improvements. That is a gain of $160,000 over 15 years!

Awesome! What compounded rate of return is this gain equivalent to? 3%. It most likely didn't even keep up with inflation. The $40,000 of taxes, insurance, upkeep, etc. over 15 years is most likely on the low side. Would you consider 3% a good rate of return?

You may be thinking that I forgot about your house appreciating in value. We assumed that all three couples live in *identical* houses that were originally worth *exactly the same* amount. The only difference is how they hold their mortgage. Which family's home will appreciate the fastest?

All three homes will appreciate at exactly the same rate! The value of their homes has absolutely nothing to do with how much they owe on their home. Making large down payments, or making extra monthly principal payments, does not make your house worth more regardless of whether you owe it all or owe nothing on your home.

Remember that the Owe It Alls borrowed $300,000. What interest rate would they have to earn in their investment over 30 years to break even? The logical guess would be 6% if that were how much their mortgage rate was originally, but the actual investment interest they would have to earn is 4.2%, assuming a 30% tax bracket. This is due to the mortgage interest deduction. In this scenario, it cost the Owe It Alls 4.2% interest for them to control their money instead of the lender having control. Therefore, if you receive a mortgage interest deduction it reduces the investment risk you would have to take for you to be in control of your own money.

Quite often I hear people say it just *feels* better having my home paid as soon as possible. Could the Owe It Alls pay their home off in the future, before the 30 years are up if they choose to? Of course! If they have been investing the difference between a 15-year mortgage payment and their 30-year mortgage payment, how many years would it take them to have enough money to pay their mortgage off?

If we ran a real-life scenario and use a 6% rate on the mortgage interest and compare apples to apples, it would take approximately 14 years and one month of investing the difference to be able pay the 30-year mortgage off. For those people who choose a 15-year mortgage to 'save interest' and pay their home off as quickly as possible, *they can do the same thing by taking a 30-year mortgage, control the money themselves and not pay any additional interest* if they choose to take the money out of their investment in 14 years to pay their mortgage off. In the meantime they had total control over their money.

What about the Pay Extras paying extra principal payments? Why did they choose a 15-year mortgage? Most people choose a 15-year mortgage because of the interest they think they will save because the perception is - the shorter the loan - the lower the cost. If that were true, then paying cash for the entire home upfront would be the best choice. We have seen that this is not the case based on the Free & Clear's who would have had to sell their home for more than $1.7 million to match the investment account of the Owe It Alls.

Often you will hear someone who chose this route say they are going to 'catch up' after they pay their mortgage off, by starting to invest all of the money, plus extra that they've been paying towards their mortgage over the last 15 years. I can tell you that when you run the numbers on this transaction they will end up with the *exact same amount* of money if they had invested the difference from the start and chosen a 30-year mortgage. There is one big difference between the two, though. *Investment risk is less over longer periods of time.* There is more risk involved in earning a rate of return over 15 years then there is over 30 year period of time.

These same people also subscribe to the financial strategy of maximizing their contributions to a tax-deferred retirement account. I will address this issue in the Investing chapter. Suffice it to say that I am not a fan of tax-deferred investment strategies.

The Post-Story Quiz

True or False

• A large down payment will save you more money on your mortgage over time, than a small down payment.

• A 15-year mortgage will save you more money than a 30-year mortgage.

• Making extra principal payments saves you money over the life of your mortgage.

• The interest rate is the *main factor* in determining the cost of a mortgage.

• You are financially more secure having your home paid off, than having it financed 100%.

Let's shift gears on these three families and ask: What is the #1 cause of someone losing their home?

A disability – by far!

How would each family be affected by an unexpected disability? If the Free and Clears are unexpectedly disabled and can no longer work, do you think they can get a loan against the equity in their home? I seriously doubt it. What bank do you know of that will loan you money against your home if you cannot go to work and pay them back? It would be the same for the Pay Extras.

How will the Owe It Alls be affected by an unexpected disability? They still owe a lot of money on their home but they chose a mortgage that allowed them the lowest payment, they invested their $300,000 **and** the difference between a 15-year mortgage and their 30-year mortgage. They have maintained liquidity, use and control over their money in a safe investment. If they are disabled they will tap that investment to pay their bills and maintain their current lifestyle until they are able to go back to work.

We could use the same projection for these three couples if each were unexpectedly unemployed. What lender have you ever heard of that would loan you money if you didn't have a job?

It could even be worse. Most mortgages have a clause that says if you miss a payment the lender has the right to 'call the loan'. If you are then unable to pay the loan off, they are authorized to sell your home for what you owe. They are not required to sell it for what it is worth and give you the equity. They are only required to sell it for what you owe to recoup their loss.

Until you make that last payment on your mortgage, all of the equity you believe to be yours is actually the lenders.

The question is not should you pay your house off as quickly as possible. The question is who should control the money- you or the bank? It is my desire for you to have the ability to pay off your home as quickly as possible. I believe that you should pick your mortgage, not let a mortgage pick you.

The mortgage that you choose is a huge decision and should be given much thought and due diligence. My preference is to have a mortgage for the longest allowed period with the lowest fixed interest rate. I strongly encourage you to seek wise council when choosing your mortgage.

The Financial Guide for Veterinarians

Chapter 9

HOW TO GET STARTED ON YOUR PLANNING

Wouldn't it be great to have a list of stuff you need to do as you approach graduation, along with what you need to do after you have graduated from vet school? Well that is exactly what this chapter is all about.

A few years ago I had meetings scheduled with 4th year veterinary students that were about to graduate. For several meetings in a row each student asked me for a 'To Do' list, for after graduation and beyond. I remember one young lady saying to me, "Look, I can follow a list if I just had one to follow." I thought that was a great idea and so I put the following information together:

TO DO LIST

1. BEFORE you make any big decisions you *must* have your monthly budget all squared away. We need to know exactly what it takes for you to afford your desired standard of living - within $100 per month.

2. I would set your 3 accounts up as described in chapter 3 as soon as you get settled into your new job. I do not expect you to fund all of these accounts quickly, but you must patiently follow the 'rules' listed in the budgeting and managing your expenses sections of this book.

3. Once you know what area you will be working in, go into a local bank and speak to the receptionist, letting them know that you are a new doctor in town and would like to set up a couple of accounts.

    a. While talking with them, ask if it's possible to meet the bank president. You just want to introduce yourself. This is a great relationship for in the future if you need a loan.

    b. Remember that banks are for-profit businesses and you will be educated on every decision they would like for you to make, so that *you* decide what you want instead of being told what you want.

4. I would start shopping for quality disability insurance with a reputable company about a month before your employment date.

5. I would start looking at places for rent in your soon-to-be town, at your earliest convenience.

    a. A great way to do this is to look online for homes that are available. Google 'property management companies' for your specific town, rather than just searching 'homes for rent'. This often leads to more results. Use the same strategy for renting that I have listed in the buying a house section in Chapter 8.

    b. Location is important. I put a premium on your safety and comfort.

    c. There is a lot to be said for not wanting to over spend - but let's be reasonable.

6. Get those 3 Accounts full, by using my recommendations earlier.

a. Once you are comfortable with your daily life, paychecks and standard of living, you should start working on a savings/retirement plan.

b. You want to start mapping out what your financial philosophy is- what do you want out of your life, your goals, etc. If you don't know, get help from someone who understands the veterinary industry.

c. As you develop these thoughts and ideas, you should create a strategy to accomplish those goals. Again – Get help!

7. Once your 3 Accounts are all set, then you are ready to start making the big decisions.

- Can I afford a house?
- How much house can I afford?
- Can I buy a new car?
- Which student loan repayment option is best for me?

General Considerations After Graduation

During the first semester of the financial elective that I help Dr. Robyn Wilborn with at Auburn University College of Veterinary Medicine, the group of 34 students became somewhat irritated at the lack of *specific* advice they were not receiving in the class. Of course, the class was not designed to give specific advice, but all discarded that sentiment. I wrote the following commentary to address their concerns and then followed it with some really good, brief recommendations.

It has become apparent that many students in this course are anxious for some sense of "what should I do in this instance" advice. It is my belief that I, and the other lecturers, would be doing you a great disservice by offering blanket advice to such a diverse group. This leads to speculation of unknown variables that will (or should) greatly affect a person's decision-making and the subsequent outcomes.

I have assembled the following bullet points for you to use as general considerations as you move from 'broke college student' to 'broke employed person'.

These generalities are meant to be thought provoking and not intended as specific financial advice. In no particular order – here is a list of good financial tips to live by:

o   Seek wise counsel in your early decisions. You need help – ask for it from people that you respect and trust.

o   Do not make any major purchases or big money decisions for at least 6 months.

o   Do not immediately start investing into any financial product or service until your budget and accounts are full.

o   Drive the car you are in for at least 12 months. It's just transportation.

o   Rent a place to live for the first year in the real world.

o   Your rent and expenses associated with the dwelling should be less than 1/3 of your gross income.

o   You should not spend more than 1/3 of your gross annual income on your place of residence, whether you are buying a home or renting.

o   Never spend money that you have not made yet.

o   Create a relationship with a 'small town bank.' How? Ask people in your church, your new job or trusted circle for recommendations. Ask people that you respect who they use as a banker.

o   Just because you meet with one of these bankers does not mean he or she is the banker for you! Be selective. All banks and bankers are not the same. Find one that fits your personality and that does not talk over your head. You need someone that explains answers to all of your questions clearly and patiently.

o   Create a relationship with an accountant. Follow the same instructions as for a banker. You pay them to serve your needs. Always remember that.

o   A key point regarding accountants: These are generally good, smart people. But it has been my experience that the overwhelming majority are *not* a great source of financial advice. They are generally not educated on giving you *long-term* financial advice. They are paid to take the numbers you give them and process them appropriately. They are looking in the rear view mirror so to speak. Accountants are not financial advisors.

o   Never invest money into anything that you do not understand. You are better off keeping it in a glass jar than placing it at risk on the advice of someone you 'trust.'

o   Create a good relationship with a financial consultant/advisor. Not a stockbroker. You don't need a stockbroker yet (if at all). Search for an advisor that you feel comfortable with. You will most likely become close to this person as the years pass, so choose wisely!

o Open a checking account for your monthly bills.

o Open a checking account for an emergency fund.

o Open a checking account that I call the Plan B Account. This account is for accumulating wealth! Money goes in to this account but never comes out unless it is for wealth accumulation. Granted – this account may be stagnant for a while, but establish it now.

o Once all of your planning accounts are full, take no less than 10% from the net of each paycheck and deposit it into your Plan B account. This is not negotiable. Period. You may have to sacrifice somewhere else to make this happen. Just do it.

o You need 3 to 6 months of your gross living expenses in a liquid, safe account to be used for emergencies only.

o If you cannot pay for a vehicle that you are purchasing, new or used, in 36 months or less – you cannot afford it.

o Limit meals outside of your home to three per week. Yes, 3 times per week. Otherwise carry a sack lunch. It's probably healthier anyway.

o Always carry renter's insurance on the contents of your apartment/rental home.

o Shop around for a property/casualty insurance company. That is the auto insurance and home insurance providers. Get quotes from all the major carriers. Don't just settle for the first one you go to. You usually get a discount if you have your residence and auto insurances with one carrier.

o Make certain the deductibles are suitable to your needs and lifestyle. The deductible is the amount you will pay if you file a claim.

o Ask that property casualty agent for a quote on a $1,000,000 Umbrella Policy. It is cheap and you need it.

o You do not need more than one credit card: One personal credit card and one business credit card - if you own your own clinic.

o Never carry a balance on a Credit Card. If you cannot pay for the items you are purchasing – in the month you purchase them – you cannot afford them.

o Credit Cards are a tool of convenience.

o You need some type of healthcare insurance. If your employer does not offer it to you as a benefit, shop around.

o I am a fan of the health cost sharing companies. My favorite of the ones that are available is Christian Healthcare Ministries.

o You need a simple Will, even though you may not think you have anything to leave if you are gone. You need a Will. I often say, "98% of all people die at some point." If you do not leave a Will, the state probates your estate. As I have said about other financial issues, if you don't have a plan I promise you, the Government does. A Will is cheap and easy to do. Almost any attorney can do it, or you can do it cheaply at legalzoom.com.

o Dave Ramsey, Suze Orman and Clark Howard are entertainers and salesmen, first and foremost. They give advice to the masses. You are a doctor. Your world is significantly different in many ways than the average consumer. Remember this.

o Give. The Principle of Giving – whether you are giving a tithe or giving to a charity – works.

o Financing anything is *generally* a bad idea, with the exception of a home. You can deduct the interest on a home mortgage.

o   You must maintain a **written budget** of your current expenses and look at it every day (Put it on the fridge, bathroom mirror, etc). Discipline yourself and stick to it!

o   A mortgage on a home for most people, in most situations, should be for the longest period of time allowable (which is usually 30 years) for the lowest interest rate a mortgage company or bank will offer you. Fixed. With as little money down as allowed. Generally.

o   Social Security is the biggest Ponzi scheme ever created. Don't count on it for your retirement.

o   Investing money into a Qualified Plan – such as a 401(k), IRA, etc. does not *'save you taxes'* as many accountants and advisors will tell you. Contributions into these types of plans do two things: 1) Defer the Tax. 2) Defer the Tax Calculation.

o   There are very few instances where you should ever lease a vehicle of any kind. In my opinion, almost never.

o   There is no Magic Bullet or Magic Strategy that will automatically work for your retirement. You cannot get rich quick.

o   Buying Term life insurance and Investing the difference is a strategy that does not work. Among other problems with this strategy - No one "invests the difference' – they *Consume* the difference.

o   There is no magic strategy to pay off your student loan. It will take discipline and a plan.

o   You must insure your #1 asset – your ability to go to work (disability insurance). That insurance should be with a quality carrier and sold to you by someone who understands your needs.

o   You get one chance to be a good steward of every dollar that passes through your hands. Plan and be prepared.

o   You will make mistakes. Learn from them.

o   Try and learn from other people's mistakes along the way. Those lessons are usually free!

o   You cannot spend more than you make.

Chapter 10

TIPS FOR VETERINARIANS FROM A NON-VET

I am not a veterinarian but I know a lot about the veterinary business and industry. I have been in dozens of veterinary clinics over the past few years and been able to look at their finances in great detail. I have looked over Profit & Loss statements, Balance Sheets, Production Reports and all other financial documents associated with a veterinary practice.

While in clinics I have been able to observe workflow, client relations, staff protocols, inventory and just about everything to do with the veterinary business.

Veterinary medicine is a *people* business. Yes, you are treating the pet but you are *doing business* with the owner. Your clients bring their pet to you and expect that you can identify and 'fix' what's wrong. They will come back to you over and over based on *how you make them feel*. I strongly encourage you to work on your people skills to be a better veterinarian.

Educating your client on what you are doing during an exam, and/or will do when their pet is not in their sight, is critical to providing a complete service to clients.

Giving an itemized bill detailing what services you have provided and how much each service costs is key to having less issues with check out. I am a huge fan of in-room check out. In most clinics the client checks out in the same area as the lobby and reception. The receptionist says, "It will be

$349.50 today." The client shouts, "For what?!?" Now everyone in the waiting area is interested in the answer.

Same scenario but the client's credit card is declined. Everyone in the lobby area is now keenly aware of what is going on and it is just embarrassing.

And of course in almost every checkout situation the pet has just been poked, handled, prodded and just wants to go home. The owner is being pulled and beaten while trying to retrieve their payment method from their wallet or purse.

Having your clients check out in the exam room solves many potential problems. In-room check out can also help reduce missed charges. I have found that the veterinary industry often has an issue with charging full value for their services. Educating the client on what services and procedures you are providing before and during the office visit, then providing a detailed bill and leaving your guilt at the door by charging for the services you provide, will increase your production dramatically!

Workflow in your hospital is key to employee production. It is critical to have protocols in place for every employee and procedure. I love having a team atmosphere in a working environment but there must be defined roles for each job description. One of the biggest 'holes' I have found in veterinary clinics is the lack of training and direction for the staff.

I am a proponent of letting Technicians do 'Tech work' as much as possible, and allowing Doctors to do 'Doc work'. Of course there are always times when the primary doc has to clean a room or take a history from the client. It is imperative for you to maximize your potential by managing your doctor time.

I believe communication from the top down is the best way to run a practice. Every successful business has great leadership. Placing your employees in positions to be productive is a sign of a well-run clinic. Regular office meetings are critical to communication with your coworkers.

Forward booking is something that the dentist industry does incredibly well and where the veterinary industry falls short. Before your client leaves your clinic, you absolutely *must* know when you are going to 'touch' that client next. Services such as PhoneTree do a great job of helping you keep a soft touch with your clients in between office visits, as well as remind them of upcoming promotions or scheduled wellness visits.

I am a big fan of monthly promotions. When I ask about promotions with vets they all say the same thing, "Well, we do dental month in February." There are so many other opportunities to promote your services and give a small discount. Senior Pet Care, Weight Management, No More Lost Pets – Micro chipping, No Hump – spay & neuters, Military appreciation, and Heartworm Awareness are just a few ideas for monthly promotions.

I like the idea of creating a 'Vaccine Fast Lane' to free up some exam room space and get those clients in and out quickly.

I love pet ID cards- love them! Pet ID cards are an easy way to offer added value to your clients. It is a constant reminder that you are their primary veterinarian and you care about their pet.

Keeping an accurate inventory is critical to a well-run veterinary practice. I see so many clinics that keep a very 'loose' inventory. It is not fun to discuss, but inventory theft by employees is happening at every veterinary clinic in America- in my opinion. I strongly encourage you to keep a tight and accurate inventory.

A properly priced wellness program can be a tremendous opportunity to promote compliance as well as make a little more money.

A client of mine has a family owned clinic, which has a real neat approach to euthanasia. Many years ago they had a custodial employee named Hank. Hank had passed away and the family wanted to honor him. When euthanasia is scheduled and the receptionist sees the client pull in the parking lot, she announces over the intercom that 'Hank is in the house.' This is a notice to everyone in the clinic that they need to hold it down for the next 30 minutes or so while a grieving client spends their last minutes with their beloved pet. What a great way to honor a beloved employee and be respectful of the grieving client.

You are in one of the most honorable professions on the planet. In many respects, you sacrificed and paid a great sum to earn a degree in a profession that you desire to be in. Very few of the veterinarians that I meet just woke up one day in their early 20's and thought, "Hey, I think I will be a veterinarian." For the overwhelming majority of you, this has been a dream from long ago.

Conclusion

Reality says that there are parts of this book that speak directly to you, and parts that are just not for you at all. My desire is that the majority of the book would be things that you can use and implement right away. I hope there is at least one item of information that brings value to your life and your professional career.

As the years unfold, I find myself with a strong feeling of protection over veterinary students and young veterinarians. It is a unique industry and there are many opportunities to be taken advantage of as you enter your career.

People generally do not bring you their pet because you are a great surgeon or have a special gift of diagnosis. They *expect* you to diagnose and 'fix' their pet properly and timely.

They bring their pet to you because of who you are and how you treat them as people. They come back because of how you make them feel. I sometimes hear a student say that they wanted to get into the veterinary business because they do not want to deal with people. I have bad news for them – you are treating the pet, but you are doing business with people. The veterinary business is a people business. Learn to enjoy those relationships.

If you are a student and have questions that you would like my help with, feel free to email me. I am happy to try and help point you in the right direction.

If you are part of a student veterinary organization, or a state veterinary association, and would like to have me come and speak to your group, please feel free to contact me.

Spending Money, Time and Emotional Currency

I often say that in this life you do not only spend money. You spend your time and you spend your emotional currency.

As you mature in your profession I strongly encourage you to spend your time wisely. There are only 24 hours in a day – even for rich people.

Likewise, you only have so much emotional currency to give to the people and things in your life. Spend it where it counts.

Family Meetings

Something that I have found over the years with families is that the adults almost never share their financial position with their children. This tends to hold true as these children become young adults with families of their own.

In 2007 I started having what I call 'Family Meetings' with my young family. If you can envision my wife and I sitting in our living room, holding court with my two-year-old, four-year-old and five-year-old. At that time we used our family meetings to spend time together, share silly thoughts and ideas with each other, and to pray together.

Fast-forward to the writing of this book and our family meetings are starting to have more mature themes. We discuss a vast array of different topics and many of them are still about our silly thoughts and ideas.

My wife and I have used these family meetings to share our family beliefs, strengthen our relationship as a family unit, and encourage open dialogue about our family's finances.

As our family matures, it is our intention to use these meetings to develop ideas that will help grow our family together. I encourage you to consider family meetings of your own in the future.

One of my favorite quotes about acquiring 'stuff' is by C.S. Lewis:

"The pain of not getting what you want is only surpassed by the pain of getting what you want and finding it's not enough." C.S. Lewis

So true! I do not really have anything to add to that, I just wanted to make sure I put it somewhere in this book.

Best of luck in your career! May all of your needs be met.
Phil: 4:19

About the Author

As referenced in Chapter 1, I became passionate about estate planning, tax strategies and helping people with their planning after I watched my dad build a business from nothing, only to have half taken in taxes after he sold out and then half again taken in estate taxes upon his death.

Since that time, I have owned significant amounts of both residential and commercial real estate. I am current owner and/or co-owner in several businesses. My client base ranges from convenience store chain owners to construction company owners, high school teachers, college basketball coaches, funeral home directors, accountants, attorneys, real estate agents, heating and air company owners, veterinary practice owners and veterinary associates.

I have clients all over the United States from Texas to upstate New York and almost every state in between. I am able to maintain a working relationship with clients regardless of where they live.

My relationship with the veterinary industry has developed over the last 10 years and I am proud to be associated with such an honorable group of people. I have been privileged to meet with and discuss the financial concerns of hundreds of veterinary students over the years and I have *never* solicited a student to become a client of mine. Not once. I believe that students need help *understanding* their options and the pros & cons, *not* to be pressured into making financial decisions. The truth is - vet students aren't making any money as a student anyway! I do have many veterinary clients at all stages of their career, although I do not work exclusively in the veterinary industry. I believe that based on my experience I am as well equipped to give consultation to people in the veterinary industry as anyone else in the country.

I am always interested in taking on new clients, but I do have specific criteria for someone interested in becoming a client of mine.

Criteria to become a client:

1)   You must be friendly.

a.   I enjoy what I do for a living and I don't care to work with people that are just not very nice. Even the rich ones. It's just no fun working with unhappy people.

2)   You must be open-minded.

a.   I am *more than happy* to explain the strategies that I offer my clients as many times as it takes for them to have clarity, and in more than one way if needed, until they fully understand what I am proposing.

b.   I *am not* willing to *defend* my position to a client's parent, brother, sister or uncle who love the financial gurus on the radio or has this 'financial thing' figured out. I have found that this just leads to hard feelings.

c.   I *am,* of course, willing to discuss my strategies with your parents, accountant and attorney. They usually need my help too.

3)   You must allow me to provide you with the products and services that I am licensed to sell if you *need* a financial product or service. Such As:

a. You *need* a Last Will and Testament. I *am not* an attorney. I cannot provide that document for you.

b. You *need* a retirement plan. I *am* licensed in just about every financial product available. Even if your brother, dad or Uncle Joe is a financial planner – our agreement will be that I get to prepare the paperwork if you use my strategies.

c. You *need* disability insurance. Even if you currently have disability insurance, it has been my experience that what most vets have is not adequate. If you and I go through your planning and *you decide* what you have is inadequate, I get to prepare the paperwork for your new disability insurance.

How much do I charge?

I do *not* currently charge clients to become a client, but I also do not take everyone as a client that desires for me to be their consultant. *(See criteria list above)* For clients within an 8-hour drive of Auburn, Alabama, I may choose to drive to meet you for the first meeting. For clients outside of that range, I may choose to do a couple of online meetings with you. Regardless of the meeting format, I like to spend about an hour and a half getting to know you and asking a lot of questions. Usually by the end of our conversation, we both can mutually agree if I should become your consultant or not. If we are a match, then I am available to you for all of your financial and veterinary industry concerns.

What exactly do I do for my clients?

The overwhelming majority of my clients use me as a sounding board for almost every major decision they are faced with. As evidenced by the statements from current clients on the back cover of this book, and in the opening pages, I am a tremendous resource for my clients. In most cases I have either experienced their situation myself or have helped clients navigate the same issue and I tap into that experience to help them.

Early in my planning process I help the client understand their current financial position and all of their potential exposure to loss of wealth. I create strategies for the client to protect what they have, as well as grow their wealth in the most protected, tax-efficient manner possible. I start by making certain that they have all of the financial documents I have noted in this book, and that they are correct and in order. I review all of their current insurances to make certain they are covered properly. I review all of their current investments and explain what the pros and cons of each investment are. I then develop a strategy specific to their wants and desires for their current position and future retirement. The overwhelming majority of my clients become friends of mine. I rarely put a plan into place and then have any less than a semi-annual review with them each year thereafter. I am also well versed in simple to complex Estate Planning. I provide my clients with life and disability insurance as well as almost every type of investment plan available.

I do not believe that traditional financial planning works. I believe in challenging the government's ability to tax everything you do that is successful. I believe in creating investment and retirement strategies for my clients where their wealth distribution at retirement is considered Cash Flow, as defined by the IRS tax code, and not classified as income – *and therefore not subject to income taxes.*

I do this by using sections of the IRS tax code that have been around for more than 100 years, using a financial product that is specifically designed to generate *tax-advantaged cash flow* in retirement. This cash flow, as defined by the IRS tax code, is not considered income and therefore off the radar of the IRS for the rest of your life.

I have successfully set up these types of tax-advantaged plans for my clients for years. In that time, my clients have not lost a single dollar based on my investment strategies. ·

I am well versed in practice location for purchase, practice purchase negotiation, purchase feasibility studies, practice valuations, practice assessment and floor plan design assessment. I am able to provide those services through my consulting company.

I am well versed in contract negotiation as described in Chapter 5. I have written several employment contracts for clients as well. If you have questions for me, you are welcome to email.

You can find us on Facebook @

The Financial Guide for Veterinarians

www.facebook.com/financialguideforveterinarians/

You can follow Ethan on Twitter

@ethandawe

You can join Innovative Financial Solutions, LLC

e-Newsletter @

www.ethandawe.com

You can email Ethan directly @

ethan@ethandawe.com

To schedule Ethan to come speak to your veterinary practice, valued corporate clients, student organization such as VBMA or SAVMA, or your state's Veterinary Medical Association, contact Ethan directly @

ethan@ethandawe.com

REFERENCES

There are references to averages, percentages and estimations throughout this book, primarily in Chapter 5. All of these references have been taken from articles and information found in publications by: AVMA, VetEcon, AAHA and other industry sources.

The Financial Guide for Veterinarians

Disclaimer: The publisher and the author make no representations or warranties with respect to the accuracy or completeness of the content of this work. No warranty may be created or extended by sales or promotional materials. The advice and strategies contained herein may not be suitable for every situation. This work is sold or given with the understanding that the author and publisher is not engaged in rendering legal, accounting, or other professional services. If professional assistance is required, the services of a competent professional person should be sought. The fact that an organization or website is referred to in this book as a citation, and/or a potential source of further information, does not mean that the author or publisher endorses the information from the organization or website. Further, readers should be aware that the Internet websites listed in this work might have changed or disappeared between when this work was written and when it is read. A great effort has been made to provide accurate and current information regarding the covered material; neither Innovative Financial Solutions LLC, nor Ethan Dawe, are responsible for any errors or omissions, or for the results obtained from the use of this information. The ideas, suggestions, general principles and conclusions presented here are subject to local, state and federal laws and regulations and revisions of same, and are intended for informational purposes only. All information in this report is provided "as is" with no guarantee of completeness, accuracy, or timeliness regarding the results obtained from the use of this information. Your use of this information is at your own risk. The reader assumes full responsibility and risk of loss resulting from the use of this information. Innovative Financial Solutions, LLC and/or Ethan Dawe will not be liable for any direct, special, indirect, incidental, consequential, or punitive damages or any other damages whatsoever, whether in an action based upon a statute, contract, or otherwise relating to the use of this information. This publication contains the opinions and ideas of its author and is designed to provide useful advice in regard to the subject matter covered. However, this publication is sold or given with the understanding that neither the author, called the publisher, is engaged in rendering legal, accounting or other professional services. If a legal advice or other expert assistance is required, the services of a competent professional should be sought. The author and publisher specifically disclaim any responsibility for liability, loss or risk, personal or otherwise, that is incurred as a consequence, directly or in directly, of the use and/or application of any of the contents of this book. In a specific repetition in various published works from the publisher or others, unless noted, is an unintentional result of the nature of financial terminology in the fairly narrow focus of the financial writing and editing in which publisher and author are involved.